Making Peace with Cancer

A FRANCISCAN JOURNEY

Making Peace with Cancer

A FRANCISCAN JOURNEY

Robert M. Stewart, O.F.M.

Foreword by Regis A. Duffy, O.F.M.

PAULIST PRESS
New York/Mahwah, N.J.

Special thanks to Fr. Servus Gieben, O.F.M. Cap. for permission to
reproduce the miniatures from the fifteenth-century manuscript of
St. Bonaventure's *Legenda maior,* which is preserved at the Franciscan
museum of the Historical Institute of the Capuchins at Rome.

Francis of Assisi's "Canticle of the Creatures" is taken from *Francis of Assisi:
Early Documents, Volume I—The Saint,* edited by Regis Armstrong, O.F.M.
Cap., Wayne Hellman, O.F.M. Conv., and William Short, O.F.M.
(Hyde Park, N.Y.: New City Press, 1999), 113.

Excerpts from St. Bonaventure's *Legenda maior,* his *Major Life of St. Francis,*
are taken from *Francis of Assisi: Early Documents, Volume II—The Founder,*
edited by Regis Armstrong, O.F.M. Cap., Wayne Hellman, O.F.M. Conv.,
and William Short, O.F.M. (Hyde Park, N.Y.:
New City Press, 2000), 525–649.

Book design by Theresa M. Sparacio & Lynn Else
Cover design by Lynn Else

Library of Congress Cataloging-in-Publication Data

Stewart, Robert M., 1950-
Making peace with cancer : a Franciscan journey /
by Robert M. Stewart.
p. cm.
ISBN 0-8091-4054-3
1. Stewart, Robert M., 1950- 2. Cancer—Patients—
Religious life. 3. Cancer—Religious aspects—Catholic Church.
4. Francis, of Assisi, Saint, 1182-1226. I. Title.

BV4910.33 .S74 2001
248.8′6196994—dc21
2001021762

Published by Paulist Press
997 Macarthur Boulevard
Mahwah, New Jersey 07430

www.paulistpress.com

Printed and bound in the United States of America

CONTENTS

To my family
who first loved me
and
spoke to me of God

ACKNOWLEDGMENTS

I would like to thank but a few of the people who have touched my life, encouraged my painting and nurtured the production of this text: Larry Boadt and the editors at Paulist Press for their encouragement and assistance in bringing this work to its final form; Barbara Carr and the other readers of my initial manuscript who encouraged me to share it in published form; the friars at St. Bonaventure University who first suggested that I write about my experience of cancer as something "beyond surviving"; the many people who read my article in *America* and expressed to me how much my own experience of cancer spoke to their hearts; Servus Gieben and my Franciscan brothers at the Capuchin Historical Institute at Rome for permission to use the illustrations from the illuminated manuscript, but more profoundly for their most gracious hospitality over the years and especially during my months of recuperation, when I began to write this text; my Franciscan brothers of Holy Name Province who formed me in the ways of Francis and thus added significant Franciscan hues to all of my painting; Mike Blastic and other friends who have sustained me throughout this journey by their own painting of love and gospel fidelity; Mom and all my family who through their love have enabled me to live and love intensely. My deepest thanks to all the people who have enabled, encouraged and mentored my own painting without canvas. I pray that they might find themselves within these pages and recognize therein my heartfelt gratitude.

Foreword

$\mathcal{M}$ost of us would prefer to "see" a life sketched out in a few rapid but telling strokes or painted in rich oils than simply to read someone's curriculum vitae. Cancer has evoked this artist's gift in Bob Stewart. As a Christian and a Franciscan friar, he has discovered the artist in himself: "I am painting a picture, painting with my life, painting without a canvas." What a wonderful metaphor for such a daunting task.

Christian autobiography is as old as Paul's Second Letter to the Corinthians and as recent as St. Thérèse of Lisieux's account of her life. What shines out in such narratives is Paul's reminder that we carry the glory of God in vessels of clay. Over the centuries, these narratives have been a source of encouragement for Christians struggling to walk the gospel way in the midst of the setbacks and crises of their lives.

One of the shortest of such spiritual autobiographies is the *Testament* of St. Francis of Assisi. As he faces Sister Death, Francis looks at the "footprints of God" (St. Bonaventure's phrase) in his life. Francis had experienced almost continual sickness and eventual blindness in the last years of his life. Even more painful was the discouraging awareness that not all friars had, or could have, the same degree of radical commitment to the gospel life that he had. But there is no self-pity or regret in the last words of the little Poor Man. His death had meaning because his life did.

It is not by accident that two of the best and most discussed plays on Broadway in the past few years have focused on people dying of cancer. Erik Erikson characterized the challenge of this final stage of life as a search for "integrity" in the Latin root sense, "making a whole of our lives." As much as people may want to hide from their mortality, they know instinctively that they must be able to make some sense out of the lives they have lived. In those Broadway plays, God does not seem to fit into their strategy for living or their approach to dying.

How different is this final search for integrity by this friar: "Over the years I have accomplished things, touched lives and been a good person. But Brother Cancer has been trying to push me to see beyond that; to understand that my response to God's love must be radical, must come from my depths and involve my total being; to risk in faith and stand naked before God so that I might know God's love and forgiveness...." Expressed differently, a play about Bob's final months of life with flashbacks of pivotal points in his earlier life would be markedly different from the two plays I have mentioned earlier. There is meaning in his life and in his death. These sketches of a life deeply lived speak more eloquently about the kingdom of God than any theological argument. If readers learn nothing else from this friar's story than the importance of finding God in their stories, they will have learned a great deal.

REGIS A. DUFFY, O.F.M.

Prologue

St. Francis of Assisi's
Canticle of the Creatures

Most High, all-powerful, good Lord,
Yours are the praises, the glory, and the honor, and all blessing,
To You alone, Most High, do they belong,
and no human is worthy to mention Your name.

Praised be You, my Lord, with all Your creatures,
especially Sir Brother Sun,
Who is the day and through whom You give us light.
And he is beautiful and radiant with great splendor;
and bears a likeness of You, Most High One.

Praised be You, my Lord, through Sister Moon and the stars,
in heaven You formed them clear and precious and beautiful.
Praised be You, my Lord, through Brother Wind,
and through the air, cloudy and serene, and every kind of
    weather,
through whom You give sustenance to Your creatures.

Praised be You, my Lord, through Sister Water,
who is very useful and humble and precious and chaste.
Praised be You, my Lord, through Brother Fire,
through whom You light the night,
and he is beautiful and playful and robust and strong.

Praised be You, my Lord, through our Sister Mother Earth,
who sustains and governs us,
and who produces various fruit with colored flowers and herbs.

Praised be You, my Lord, through those who give pardon for
    Your love,
and bear infirmity and tribulation.
Blessed are those who endure in peace
for by You, Most High, shall they be crowned.

Praised be You, my Lord, through our Sister Bodily Death,
from whom no one living can escape.
Woe to those who die in mortal sin.
Blessed are those whom death will find in Your most holy will,
for the second death shall do them no harm.

Praise and bless my Lord and give Him thanks
and serve Him with great humility.

$\mathcal{M}$any months have passed since I was first asked, "How did you get 'there'?" Nevertheless, the moment remains etched in memory. On Mount La Verna, the hallowed ground close to the place where Francis received the stigmata, words became sacred. Looking out upon the valley below, chilled by the wind but warmed by friendship, a friend and I spoke for hours about family and friends, about our hopes and struggles, joys and sorrows. Words became sacred because heart spoke to heart.

That moment is powerfully present for me. I can still feel his pain as he spoke about his failed marriage, the ache in his heart as he described his former spouse, the gentleness of spirit as he admitted his loneliness and love for her amid confusion, his courage and love as he told me about the loving family he hopes someday to have. I still feel his compassion and concern as I told him my cancer had spread, and he gently took my hand and, looking into my eyes, promised his prayers. I remember the tears of joy we shared as we embraced. We spoke, too briefly, about the presence of God, the call to love, the gift of peace. The moment remains, and I still hear him speaking about the peace he sensed within me and asking, "How did you get 'there'?"

Others have posed the same question, if phrased differently. At times, the question suggests a desperate search for a simple formula or process to find peace in suffering. However, the question has often emerged from deep compassion and revealed an intense desire to know God and to live fully—as with my friend amid the pain of a love lost, as with my hospital roommate who fearfully awaited surgery. Yet, as much as I wanted to respond to his question, as much as I wanted to offer something helpful for the struggle, I had no easy answer.

That night at La Verna, I told my friend that I responded to cancer as I have responded to other problems and suffering in my life. He was not satisfied and asked me to explain what I meant. For many months I have wanted to respond adequately to his question about how I've found peace with cancer, to explain better to all who ask. Therefore, I decided to write, with the hope that these words will be an adequate response for my friends who seek to understand how I found peace, and perhaps help others.

When my friend asked me how I could live with peace as cancer spread within me, I told him it is part of a larger picture. Recently, I realized that this is an image I could develop into a framework for my thoughts—I am painting a picture, painting with my life, painting without canvas.

I want to rephrase the question to "How did you learn to paint like that?" Those who have asked did not use those words, but the question is, in effect, about my background and training. Reflecting on the "canvas" on which I paint, wondering about the background that allows me to find peace, immediately brings to mind the people who have shaped the person who now "paints."

These pages will attempt to describe the development of the inner artist: my vision, faith and life. My preparation and training can only be described by remembering some of the people who formed me, who shared their love and faith, who encouraged or empowered me to live or to paint this way.

As a friar, I see the world and interpret my experience in Christian terms; I understand the gospel through a Franciscan lens. I attempt to live the gospel, "to follow the teaching and the footprints of our Lord Jesus Christ," according to the example of Francis.

Thus, when the doctors first told me that I had cancer, when they performed the first surgery and when they told me the tumor was malignant, I naturally turned to Francis. Only when they said that it could spread throughout my whole body in three to six months did I look more closely at Francis of Assisi. Only a few months before his own death, seriously ill and suffering great pain, Francis had added a verse to his "Canticle of the Creatures" praising God and celebrating "Sister Death." I wondered how he could welcome death as "sister."

The Francis to whom I turned, the Francis who now accompanies me on this journey, is different from the one I first knew or imagined. I had—as do most people—a romanticized image of him. I had heard the stories from the tradition known as the

Fioretti or "Little Flowers." Those stories—taming the wolf of Gubbio, talking with animals—define the popular image of Francis: the holy, humble, poor saint who communicates with animals and performs miracles. I pictured Francis as a saint of joy and peace, one who loved all creatures and rejoiced in all creation. Certainly, we can say that he was a man of peace and joy who loved all creatures. But some of the early legends need to be read as symbolic representations of Francis's activity: the taming of the wolf representing the reconciliation he effected between robbers and the people of Gubbio, his preaching to birds expressing how he sought out and communed with the little ones of the earth. Even after rereading some of these stories, a fully and powerfully human Francis does not emerge easily. Rather, he remains aloof, a saint to be praised, not the earthy, passionate, joyful, caring, committed and courageous man of faith who invites us to follow in the footprints of our Lord Jesus Christ and challenges us to a radical living of the gospel.

Both of these different understandings of Francis—the exalted saint and loving human—are in Giotto's image of Francis preaching to the birds. On one level, Francis appears as a nature mystic, one who mysteriously communes with animals, one with supernatural powers. However, from another perspective one finds a different Francis: the humble servant who moves with open embrace toward the little ones, in contrast to the rigid friar and unbending tree in the background; the simple, ordinary, sensitive person who has so tasted the love of God revealed in the human Jesus that he is moved to an extraordinary response of love. This Francis found God in the concrete and ordinary, lived and loved intensely, and helps me to paint without canvas. I hope to capture this Francis in these pages.

Though I plan to talk about both the life of St. Francis and my own experience, this is neither Francis's biography nor my autobiography. I mean to highlight a few important events in Francis's life and some significant experiences in my life—enough to suggest how my experience and vision have been shaped and thus evoke a sense of my journey with cancer. Further, I hope that these words might encourage reflection on the search for peace. Most profoundly, I hope that they might invite a more deliberate response to new experiences, a more conscious "painting without canvas" and—as I hope to explain in what follows—intensified living and loving.

The image of Francis preaching to the birds comes from the thirteenth-century series of frescoes attributed to Giotto that are in the upper basilica of St. Francis in Assisi. They are based on the *Major Life of St. Francis* written by St. Bonaventure in 1260. In his prologue, Bonaventure wrote: "I feel that I am unworthy and unequal to the task of writing the life of a man so venerable and worthy of imitation."

Although I set about the meager labor of sharing my own experience and vision of Francis, Bonaventure's sentiments echo within me. It is with

fear and trepidation that I proceed. I am no Francis—
I am one of his humble sons who awaits the intimate
union with God that he experienced. Yet, through
Francis I have been blessed, and I want to share that
blessing with others. I will attempt to speak about my
experience of cancer and of grace as Francis has
helped me to see it. I hope that my limited understanding and brief glimpses of grace, however inadequate, might help my readers enter more fully into the
mystery of God, perhaps through struggles and suffering—accompanied by the man from Assisi.

Apprenticed to Artists

Francis Refusing and Then Giving Alms to a Beggar.

There was a man
in the city of Assisi,
named Francis
whose memory is held in benediction,
because God graciously
preceded him with blessings of sweetness,
mercifully snatching him from the dangers of the present life,
and richly filling him with gifts of heavenly grace.

For at a young age, he lived among foolish children of mortals and was brought up in foolish ways. After acquiring a little knowledge of reading and writing, he was assigned to work in a lucrative merchant's business. Yet with God's protection, although he indulged himself in pleasures, even among wanton youths, he did not give himself over to the drives of the flesh; not even among greedy merchants did he place his hope in money or treasures, although he was intent on making a profit.

There was to be sure, growing with him from his infancy, a generous care for the poor divinely implanted in the heart of the young Francis. It had so filled his heart with kindness that, even at that time, he resolved not to be a deaf hearer of the Gospel but to give to everyone who begged, especially if he asked out of "divine love."

On one occasion, however, when he was caught up in the pressures of business, contrary to his usual manner of acting, he sent away empty-handed a poor man who had begged alms for the love of God. Immediately turning back to his heart, he ran after him, and, gently with extravagant alms, he promised God that from that moment, while he had the means, he would not refuse those who begged from him for the love of God. He observed this with untiring piety until his death and merited an abundant increase of grace and love for God. For afterwards, when he had put on Christ perfectly, he would say that even while he was in secular attire, he could scarcely ever hear any mention of the divine love without being deeply moved in his heart.

At the same time, the sensitivity of his gentleness, together with a refined set of manners, a patience and affability beyond human decorum and a generosity beyond his means singled him out as a young man of flourishing natural disposition. This seemed to be a prelude to the even greater abundance of God's blessings that would be showered on him in the future. Indeed a certain exceptionally simple man of Assisi, whom, it is believed, God had instructed, whenever he chanced to meet Francis going through the city, used to take off his cloak and spread the garment under his feet, claiming that Francis was worthy of reverence, since he was destined to do great things in the near future and would be magnificently honored by the entire body of the faithful.

—Bonaventure, *Legenda maior* I:1

Where did Francis learn such "generous care for the poor"? What in Francis's background led him to treat others with such gentleness and generosity and how might it give us the key to his journey to peace through suffering? Unfortunately, the early sources for his life give very little information about his youth. The first life, written by Thomas of Celano for Francis's canonization, depicts a vain and foolish young man who "miserably wasted and squandered his time almost up to the twenty-fifth year of his life." The later account by Bonaventure portrays him as a good, generous and virtuous young man destined for greater things and recognized as such by a simple man from the town of Assisi who prophetically laid his cloak on the ground before him. These accounts present very different images of Francis. Was he a vain and rowdy child or a virtuous and joyful youth?

These thirteenth-century sources do not give us easy answers to questions about Francis. Nevertheless, we are able—and we need—to speak about what he did, said and believed. Through study of the texts, the milieu from which each arose and their context in terms of Francis's own writings, we can deduce some historical information. I want to talk about Francis because he colors my own life. How can we understand his heart, experience, feelings, faith and vision, in order to understand his journey, his own movement to peace amid suffering?

His father, Pietro di Bernardone, a wealthy cloth merchant in Assisi, apprenticed Francis and his brother Angelo in his shop. Early accounts suggest that he was generous with his son, equipped him to go off to battle as a knight and provided for his feasts with his friends. However, Pietro's generosity had limits. As we will see, Francis changed beyond what his father could imagine or accept.

Francis's mother, a Frenchwoman named Pica, though briefly mentioned in the accounts, emerges as loving and compassionate. When Pietro put Francis in chains, Pica freed him; when Pietro sought to drag Francis back to "reality," Pica tried to support him and may even have brought him food when he was in hiding.

Both Pietro and Pica loved their son, even though a wedge was driven between father and son by Francis's choice of poverty. Francis was joyful, compassionate, sensitive, generous, kind and dramatic: he sang in French, donated his clothes and horse to a poor knight, broke his fast so that a starving young friar would not be embarrassed eating, begged alms for the poor and ministered among the lepers, revered even corrupt priests, and used dramatic gestures like stripping naked in the square in front of the bishop to give everything back to his father. Francis seems to have been integrated in his affections, which suggests that he was loved in his early youth.

Knowing that we are loved frees us to pursue our dreams. Love freed Francis to pursue his dream of knighthood, Lady Poverty, and the God revealed in Christ crucified. But before we get to the changes in Francis's life and his new pursuits, let me speak about my own background, the love, faith and openness that I experienced within my family, all of which formed my foundation and freed me to pursue dreams and to seek Christ.

My earliest memories of my father are happy: family picnics, singing together at the piano, all of us ice skating together, and "horsy rides" around the apartment. He was also strict, in my opinion *too* strict, so we had our disagreements during my high school years. He had raised all of us to be independent, but when we were, he didn't know how to respond. Our arguments peaked during the summer after my sophomore year at college. We didn't resolve things, and when I left for school, I did not intend ever to come home again. However, something happened during that year. Dad changed dramatically. He never spoke about what happened; I never asked him about it. But I am grateful that he did change, and that we again talked. The day after I arrived home from my junior year of college, one day before he died of a massive heart attack, he told me how proud he was that I would be the first Stewart to finish college. Then he said what we all want and need to hear, words that did not fall easily from my father's lips: "I love you."

There were times during our battles when I doubted his love, but these words shortly before his death erased any remaining doubt within me. Both his love and his hesitance to express that love freely have affected who I am and how I live. I want all the people that I love to know it, to hear me speak the words "I love you" often and long before my death.

My mother gave life to me in the fullest sense. Mom has carried me in her womb, in her arms and in her heart. She has always loved me—and all of us—so freely and fully that I have always felt much loved and accepted by her. She is an example of the unconditional love we find in the gospel. Her love finds its source in God, because she has shared with me her faith, her love for God.

Loving parents would have been blessing enough, but I have also felt loved by the rest of my family, particularly my grandparents. An evening that I spent with my grandfather symbolizes their love for me, a love that remains deep within me.

When I was about eight years old, my grandmother broke her hip and had to stay in the hospital for a few days. That evening Mom told me that Grandpa had asked her if I could stay overnight with him in their apartment in the building next door. In forty-seven years of marriage, he had never spent a night alone. When I arrived, Grandpa suggested that we go to the store. We went to the corner deli, where he bought a six-pack of beer for himself and said, "Get whatever you want, Bobby." I asked tentatively, "Ice cream…and soda?" He assured me that I could get *whatever* I wanted. We did not often get such treats, only on special occasions or when we had company. I placed my treasures on the counter, and he patted my head and paid the bill. Hand in hand, we walked back to his apartment.

Grandpa turned on the television in the living room and opened a beer. I decided to make an ice cream soda and scooped out a big helping of ice cream, poured a tall glass of soda, brought them out to the living room and placed them on the arm of the sofa. I took a large spoonful of ice cream and dumped it in the soda, never thinking that it would foam. But it did—all over the arm of the couch. As my ice cream soda soaked into the couch, I timidly raised my eyes and tried to prepare for the reprimand. But as I looked up into Grandpa's eyes, I saw a twinkle, found a smile and heard him say: "Don't worry about it, Bobby. We can clean it up."

Everything about him—his relaxed manner, his gentle voice, his loving eyes—spoke acceptance and love. There was no judgment for what I had done, only love and joy that I was there with him. It was just a simple, silly moment, but it lives on within me. It was one moment in their lifetime of loving, accepting and encouraging me.

My family also nurtured my life of faith. We all went to Catholic grammar school and high school, but it was the faith we shared at home that touched my heart. We went to church as a family, and we prayed at home as a family. We had family traditions, like prayers before meals and prayers together before bed, and rituals for celebrating Thanksgiving, Christmas and Easter.

We always decorated our tree together on Christmas Eve. When we were done, we gathered around Dad at the foot of the tree, and he would read us the Christmas story. He talked to us about God's love, the gift of his Son and the meaning of Christmas. Then he and Mom tucked us into bed. We never understood why they didn't want to get up right away when we woke them at dawn. We didn't realize until years later that they had had hours of work before them after we went to bed: rearranging ornaments, assembling toys and wrapping gifts. By small things like this, they transmitted love and faith to me, the foundation that has enabled me to live with intensity and passion.

When I was diagnosed with cancer, I spoke with my family about my prognosis, my faith and our love. When I thought about my own death—perhaps for the first time concretely—fear rose within me that I might predecease my mother. I didn't want her to suffer the pain of having to bury her own child. However, my death is beyond my control, and so I spoke with Mom about my death, my fear and how she views her own death. We spoke about our faith and how we both see death in terms of the promise of resurrection. Not only do we share love and faith, but we are able to speak openly and honestly about our lives and our deaths, our fears and hopes. That is a priceless gift!

Through the years we have laughed and cried together, have always been there for each other, have shared the secrets of our hearts as best friends, always honest and gentle and loving. Not long ago, when we celebrated our sister Patti's fiftieth birthday, each of us wrote her a letter and then shared them together. Jeanne had written:

> The one most painful experience of my life—my divorce and losing my kids—was the time I leaned on you so heavily and you were there for me. As you always are. You supported me through my anger and depression, when I'm sure it would have been much easier to walk away from the abuse and the monotony of hearing it over and over again. How can I ever thank you for all of that love, that time, that caring and that gentle understanding? I am blessed not only to know you, but also to have you as a sister and a friend.

The love, the honesty, the closeness that I experience in my family empowers me. An insight I had after my first surgery, when I was in the midst of radiation therapy, illustrates this. As I limped into the hospital and queued up at the central desk with the other patients, I looked at the long line that stretched before me and realized that I was the only one standing alone. Everyone else was accompanied by a spouse, parent, friend or relative. I stood there—as I had each day—alone. But I realized that I did not *feel* alone. The love I felt from my family, as well as from my Franciscan family and friends, accompanied me at each step. Their love and support so surrounded me in my solitude that I never felt alone. That morning, as I stood in line and became conscious of their love and presence, I began to pray in gratitude for the blessing of family, friends, brothers—for the blessing of love in my life.

Mentored by Masters

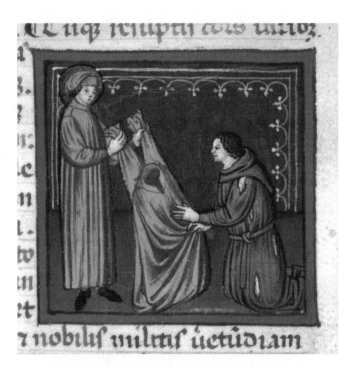

Francis Clothing a Poor Knight.

Because affliction can enlighten spiritual awareness,
the hand of the Lord was upon him,
and a change of the right hand of the Most High,
afflicting his body with prolonged illness
in order to prepare his soul for the anointing of the Holy Spirit.

And when the strength of his body was restored, dressed as usual in his fine clothes, he met a knight who was of noble birth, but poor and badly clothed. Moved by a pious impulse of care for his poverty, he took off his own garments and clothed the man on the spot. At one and the same time he fulfilled the two-fold duty of piety by covering over the embarrassment of a noble knight and relieving the want of a poor human being.

The following night, when he had fallen asleep, the divine kindness showed him a large and splendid palace with military arms emblazoned with the insignia of Christ's cross. Thus it vividly indicated that the mercy he had exhibited to a poor knight for love of the supreme King would be repaid with an incomparable reward. When he asked to whom these belonged, the response he received from on high was that all these things were for him and his knights.

Therefore, on waking up in the morning, since he was not yet disciplined in penetrating the divine mysteries and did not know how to pass through the visible appearance to contuit the invisible truth, he assessed the unusual vision to be a judgment of great prosperity in the future. For this reason, still ignorant of the divine plan, he set out to join a generous count in Apulia, hoping in his service to obtain the glory of knighthood, as his vision foreshadowed.

Shortly after he had embarked on his journey and had gone as far as the neighboring city, he heard the Lord speaking to him during the night in a familiar way: "Francis, who can do more for you, a lord or a servant, a rich person or one who is poor?" When Francis replied that a lord and a rich person could do more, he was at once asked: "Why, then, are you abandoning the Lord for a servant and the rich God for a poor mortal?" And Francis replied: "Lord, what do you want me to do?" And the Lord answered him: "Go back to your own land, because the vision which you have seen prefigures a spiritual outcome which will be accomplished in you not by a human but by a divine plan."

When morning came, then, he returned in haste to Assisi, free of care and filled with joy, and, already made an exemplar of obedience, he awaited the Lord's will.

From that time on, as he was removing himself from the pressure of public business, he would eagerly beg the divine kindness to show him what he should do. When the flame of heavenly desire intensified in him by the practice of frequent prayer, and already, out of his love for a heavenly home, he despised all earthly things as nothing; he realized that he had found a hidden treasure, and, like a wise merchant, planned to buy the pearl he had found by selling everything.

Nevertheless,
how he should do this, he did not yet know;
except that it was suggested to his spirit
that a spiritual merchant must begin with contempt for the world
and a knight of Christ with victory over one's self.
—Bonaventure, *Legenda maior*, I:2–4

I wish we knew what was going on within Francis during those early years, but the thirteenth-century sources do not describe his interior changes. Rather, they highlight some of the experiences that were significant in his development or conversion. For example, we know that when Francis was about twenty, he went off to battle, only to be defeated and imprisoned in Perugia. His father arranged for his release a year later by paying a ransom.

Francis returned to Assisi and spent a year convalescing. The experience changed Francis. No longer lord of the feasts, no longer the eager apprentice in his father's shop, he wandered and wondered, but the path before him remained unclear. It is comforting and encouraging that Francis—the great saint of Assisi who has had a profound effect on countless people throughout the centuries—took years to understand and respond to God's call.

What changed Francis? What moved him from his desire to be a great knight? What most touched his heart, raised new questions, suggested new directions, opened new vision? We can only speculate. Was his time in prison a life-altering "near death" experience? Did he see some of his friends die in battle? Was he himself wounded, and did he suffer from infection and disease? In the squalor of a medieval prison, in the midst of death and suffering, did he question the senselessness of war and the meaning of life?

Francis returned to Assisi in a weakened physical state; an imposed convalescence would force him to reflect further on suffering, life, meaning and peace. But nothing became immediately clear for Francis. He dreamed of a palace full of arms and misinterpreted it as confirmation of his desire for knighthood.

Francis once again readied himself as a knight and joined William of Brienne's army. We do not know what changed Francis's heart, only that he returned to Assisi and abandoned his quest for knighthood. The news of William's death in battle could have reached Spoleto at about the same time as Francis—a possible explanation for his decision to return home. Perhaps being confronted by death made him reassess his life. He would spend more time searching and praying, seeking deeper meaning and experience. His childhood, his apprenticeship in his father's shop at Assisi, his quest for knighthood, his formation within a Christian culture, his encounter with different people and ideas, his experience of battle and illness and undoubtedly his dialogue with others, all coalesced to make the young Francis desire to know and live the truth.

Experiences and encounters in my life have coalesced to bring me to seek a deeper religious commitment by following Francis in his order of lesser brothers. I am encouraged by the slowness of Francis's conversion, precisely because my own journey has taken so long. Having been a Franciscan for years, I am embarrassed to admit that I have only recently begun to understand Francis more fully: in and through cancer.

One of the most significant experiences in my journey was a class called Interpersonal Relations taught by Miss Manock, who was the strongest and gentlest woman I had ever met. My friends in the nursing school (which at that time was almost entirely women) had spoken often about the class, how it had challenged and transformed them. I was intrigued. Although I was in the School of Arts and Sciences, I decided to try to get into the course.

There was only one coed section of the course, so I decided to ask Miss Manock about getting into that section. She said yes. I thanked her. We spoke briefly, and as I turned to leave her office, she said warmly, "See you next Tuesday."

The following Tuesday I was excited as I walked down the corridor to the classroom. But when I got to the door, my excitement changed to fear. I looked in and saw only women. I was too embarrassed to enter. I paused for an instant and turned to continue down the hall, just to have a moment to think. It was too late. Miss Manock had spotted me at the door and immediately called out: "Get in here."

I whispered to Miss Manock that she had told me that the Tuesday section was coed. She smiled and said, "It is *now*."

And so began an extremely important chapter in my life: twenty-four women, Miss Manock and me. Only years later would I recognize that encounter as one of the most critical and significant moments in my journey. In class, each of us had to describe and analyze our own psychopathology. After much painful soul-searching, in front of twenty-four young women, I tried to explain how I structured distance into my relationships, why I kept others from seeing and knowing who I was. I realized that I did not like or accept myself fully. I knew that I was intelligent, but I was not a good athlete. I had never earned a varsity letter, so I felt inadequate, unattractive and incomplete.

Miss Manock asked my classmates, those twenty-four young women, to talk about my looks. I wanted to crawl behind the blackboard. They said words like "good looking" and even "gorgeous." I heard the words, but I couldn't accept them or believe them about myself. My homework included writing a letter to my father in order to heal our relationship, talking openly about my inner thoughts and feelings with *everyone* for a few weeks, and having a heart-to-heart talk with one of the women in the class every week. Every Tuesday I witnessed Miss Manock's profound insight, skillful analysis and effective counsel. I trusted her wisdom, and so with fierce commitment I attempted to do all of my homework.

In those brief months Miss Manock catalyzed immense growth within me; she offered me insights and suggested new ways for me to relate to others that freed me. I became more aware of my feelings and freer to express them to others; I began to discover the most precious part of the person, the heart, and I learned how to express the spontaneous inner responses of joy, love, laughter, affection.

At that time I wasn't sure that I even believed in God. When I went home for vacations, I would not go to church, to the chagrin of my parents. But then I met Miss Manock—a woman of deep, intense faith. She expressed her faith freely and lived it boldly. Because of my encounter with such a powerful, grace-filled embodiment of gentleness and strength, I found myself searching again for the God I had known, the God who gave such strength to Miss Manock, the Love that empowered her to be so gentle, the God who had given meaning to my life, the Love that is the source of all life.

I knew even then that my "Miss Manock experience" would color the rest of my life. I know now that she helped free my heart to enter more fully into life and love, that she invited me to live more intensely. I became—though at that time could not have named it—more "Franciscan," more intense in my search for God, more aware of God in the ordinary, better able to accept myself and more free to serve others. Miss Manock invited us all to make things fun, to make the best of any situation, to speak the truth, to share our love, to express our emotions—to speak to people *now* about their goodness since, as she would say, "A rose to the living is worth garlands to the dead." In all these things, Miss Manock taught me, implicitly, how to deal with cancer.

Two years later I graduated and began teaching science at a Catholic high school. I loved teaching and at the time couldn't imagine anything more satisfying, exciting and enjoyable. Yet, at moments I would feel a lack deep within me, as if there were a tiny leak that needed to be filled in the wall of a great dam. I believed that I might plug that hole within me with a deeper religious commitment. I wondered and searched.

I began to think about the priesthood, but I didn't think I could live such a solitary life. It became a possibility for me when I met a group of Franciscans in a parish in New Jersey, about an hour from where I was teaching. Those friars seemed to work twenty hours a day, yet they exuded a palpable and attractive joy. They showed great concern for each other—they were joyful, hardworking brothers! I came to believe that I might be able to live a deeper religious commitment in a group like that.

I began a conversation with those friars that led to my entering the Franciscans at a pre-novitiate house in the Bronx at the end of the summer, just to "give it a shot." Though my Franciscan journey has not been without its ups and downs, doubts and difficulties, the life seemed to fit me, seemed to be the path to which I was called. I continued through novitiate, formation, graduate studies, ordination, ministries and then doctoral studies. My life took on a different shape. I would need to learn about prayer and community, about praying in common and being a brother.

These years of learning, of being formed in the Franciscan vision and life, would build upon and become as important as my experiences of love and faith in my family, as well as my Miss Manock-mentored growth as a person. My Franciscan formation has shaped who I am and how I see the world. My understanding of God and my experience of prayer have influenced my response to this cancer within me.

In order to explain how I've found peace, I must describe my prayer—my relationship or way of relating to God. It is a very important part of my life. I can't imagine how I would respond to cancer without it. Most people—surprisingly, most Franciscans and other religious—don't talk much about their personal prayer. Perhaps it is too difficult to be open and honest about something so intimate. It is difficult even with close friends. But our prayer is too essential to who we are and how we respond to difficulties in life *not* to talk about it. It becomes more obvious in times of illness.

My prayer has changed over the years, and I pray differently at different times. What remains constant is my desire to know God more deeply, more intimately. I believe the way to come to know God— as Francis found—is through Christ. And so, my prayer involves reading the gospels, picturing Jesus, and attempting not only to speak to but also to listen to the Lord.

Perhaps relating one experience will better describe my prayer—one in the very ordinary, mundane, but incarnational moment of jogging. Several years ago, I was invited to spend two weeks in the Holy Land. I spent eleven days at the Spiritual Center at Tabgha, along the shore of the Sea of Galilee. The days were filled with quiet solitude, prayer and meditation, and I was engulfed by the sounds of the sea, the songs of the birds, the rhythms of the wind and the waves. What a gift and blessing to climb the Mount of the Beatitudes, to walk along the shore of the Sea of Galilee, to live where Jesus had preached and ministered, where he had gathered his disciples and shared his life with them.

Each day I rose early, before the scorching sun, and ran along a deserted road that parallels the sea on its northern shore, past the ruins of Capharnaum, down toward Bethsaida. On my return I looked up toward the Mount of the Beatitudes. As I ran, I surveyed the hillsides, watching strange animals dart about the rocks, noting the contours of the rocky terrain, listening to the sounds of the sea and birds of the air. I imagined fishermen along the shore tending their nets, huddled together, talking about their catch, the sea, the weather, and discussing what they had heard about Jesus.

To my surprise, I began to identify with Peter and began to imagine his initial contact with the man from Nazareth: the first time he heard this Jesus, then meeting him along the shore, talking with him while cleaning his nets, struggling to understand the meaning of Jesus' parables and puzzling over his own strange attraction to him. I wondered about Peter's response to Jesus, his struggle to understand so different a man: a laborer whose calloused hands offered gentleness and compassion, a Galilean whose common language and ordinary images spoke to his heart, a carpenter whose vision focused more on people and justice, a preacher whose parables left him confused and unsettled, a Jew whose faith and commitment humbled him, a man whose friendship was a gift beyond price.

The Peter of my imagination did manual work, spoke boldly, felt passionately, acted impulsively, and after meeting Jesus, felt a profound, almost painful yearning. Peter—a good man, faithful friend, dedicated worker—heard Jesus speak and struggled in confusion. His life had been set; he felt secure on his way, yet this man had touched him. He could not explain why he felt so driven, why he desperately needed to see Jesus again, to listen to his words. His eyes searched the countryside as he walked; his pace quickened and his heart beat more rapidly as he hastened to find him. He found himself running, sweating in the morning heat, panting almost as a sense of urgency grew: where could Jesus have gone, where would he be staying…?

Peter became real for me as I jogged along the road, eyes searching, soul seeking, longing, running after Jesus—wanting to hear his message, to be in his presence, to understand better the sense of call building within me. It was a profound experience of being called to follow. I would return to that moment often.

Back in the States, jogging along familiar paths, searching different landscapes, I again felt that yearning to see the Lord. Far from Galilee but close to Peter, I longed to hear the Lord's call, to sense his presence. Even after surgery, when I was unable to walk, beyond a desire to jog, that same intense search emerged, a desperate longing to know how the Lord was calling me to follow. The experience remained with me and helped me to approach cancer as a "jogger," as one running after the Lord, searching to find God in the ordinary experiences of my life, to find God and to know how I am being called to follow in and through illness.

Sketching the Scene

Francis Embracing a Leper.

One day, therefore, while he was riding his horse through the plain that lies below the city of Assisi, he met a leper. This unforeseen encounter struck him with not a little horror. Recalling the plan of perfection he had already conceived in his mind, and remembering that he must first conquer himself if he wanted to become a knight of Christ, he dismounted from his horse and ran to kiss him. As the leper stretched out his hand as if to receive something, he gave him money with a kiss. Immediately mounting his horse, however, and turning all around, even though the open plain stretched clear in all directions, he could not see the leper anywhere. He began, therefore, filled with wonder and joy, to sing praises to the Lord, while proposing, because of this, to embark always on the greater.

He then began to seek out solitary places, favorable to grieving, where, with unutterable groans, he concentrated incessantly on meriting to be heard by the Lord after the long perseverance of his prayers.

One of those days, withdrawn in this way, while he was praying and all of his fervor was totally absorbed in God, Christ Jesus appeared to him as fastened to a cross. His soul melted at the sight, and the memory of Christ's passion was so impressed on the innermost recesses of his heart. From that hour, whenever Christ's crucifixion came to his mind, he could scarcely contain his tears and sighs, as he later revealed to his companions when he was approaching the end of his life. Through this the man of God understood as addressed to himself the Gospel text: If you wish to come after me, deny yourself and take up your cross and follow me.

From then on he clothed himself with a spirit of poverty, a sense of humility, and an eagerness for intimate piety. For previously not only had association with lepers horrified him greatly, so too did even gazing upon them from a distance. But, now because of Christ crucified, who according to the text of the prophet appeared despised as a leper, he, in order to despise himself completely, showed deeds of humility and humanity to lepers with a gentle piety. He visited their houses frequently, generously distributed alms to them, and with a great drive of compassion kissed their hands and their mouths.

To poor beggars he even wished to give not only his possessions but his very self, sometimes taking off his clothes, at others altering them, at yet others, when he had nothing else at hand, ripping them in pieces to give to them.

To poor priests he also provided help, reverently and piously, especially in the appointments of the altar, and, in this way, he both became a participant in the divine worship and provided assistance for the need of its celebrants.

With religious devotion he visited at this time the shrine of the Apostle Peter. When he saw a large number of the poor before the entrance of the church, led partly by the gentleness of his piety, encouraged partly by the love of poverty, he gave his own clothes to one of the neediest among them. Dressed in his rags, he spent that day in the midst of the poor with an unaccustomed joy of spirit, in order to spurn worldly glory and to arrive, by ascending in stages, at Gospel perfection.

> He was more attentively vigilant
> to mortifying his flesh
> so that he might carry externally in his body
> the cross of Christ
> which he carried internally in his heart.
> The man of God, Francis,
> did all these things
> while not yet withdrawn from the world
> in attire and way of life.
> —Bonaventure, *Legenda maior*, I:5–6

*F*rancis's encounter with the leper played an important role in his journey. Indeed, the event was so foundational for him that he begins his Testament by recalling how it began his conversion. He emerged from it with a new vision, determined purpose and clearer direction. Francis's embrace of the leper, which had already been meaningful and central in my own life, more recently has spoken powerfully to my heart.

Early Franciscan iconography preserves not this encounter with the leper but Francis receiving the stigmata. Yet he cites this concrete human encounter, rather than a mystical experience, as having the most significance in the beginning of his conversion. The meeting with the leper would color the rest of his life as he continued to search for God, to run after the Lord. But as powerful as this experience was for Francis in hindsight, he did not immediately understand its meaning and consequences.

As for me, Francis's insight has begun to make sense. Through suffering, I have begun to taste this mystery. It is frustrating that it has taken so long, that it has taken cancer to make me see more clearly. But coming to know God more in and through this has helped me to understand Francis's experience and how, or why, he could embrace suffering. However, I only have *begun* to understand—often I still struggle to embrace suffering, as did Francis.

It was difficult for me to understand, much less to accept and integrate cancer into my life. I was in good health; I kept physically fit. I jogged, worked out or played racquetball most days. I never thought my body would tire or wear out.

I pushed my body hard. I expected it to do what I wanted. I wasn't expecting a slowdown, much less a breakdown, of my body. The day before the first surgery, I ran about eight miles, assuming that I wouldn't be able to run for three or four weeks. Ten days before the beginning of the fall semester, I entered the hospital for what I thought would be a simple procedure. Given my good physical condition, the biopsy report of a low-grade cancer and my confidence in my surgeons, I not only expected to walk out of the hospital unassisted but also to teach my full load of classes one week later.

The day after, my surgeon, Dr. Mindell, explained what had been done to my leg during the operation, which was much more extensive than planned. He mentioned something about taking a month to recover, and I immediately responded, "I can't. I begin teaching in one week." Though I could tell he disagreed, he did not argue with me but said that we would talk about it in a couple of days.

When I stood up for the first time, I realized why he hadn't bothered arguing. Even given my high pain threshold, I thought I might pass out. The intense pain in my leg was a more convincing argument than the doctor could have mustered. But being thick and stubborn, I did not let reality get in the way; I conceded only that I would have to begin teaching a week late.

Five days later, two of my Franciscan brothers drove up to Buffalo to bring me home. Even though I had to hobble to the van on crutches, needed to keep my leg elevated, and was unable to sleep for more than an hour because of the pain, I still believed that I could begin teaching in a week and a half, at most two weeks. Later that week, I received some news that made a final, irrefutable argument against this point of view.

As I lay in my room amid the newly acquired appointments of crutches, walker, bandages and solutions—I tried to figure out how I could negotiate the first weeks of class. My thoughts were interrupted by a phone call. I recognized Dr. Mindell's voice before he identified himself. He had just received the full pathology report on the tissue they had removed from my leg, and it did not confirm what the biopsy had suggested was "low-grade cancer." Rather, it indicated a very aggressive form of cancer. Although he originally had suggested only surgery, both he and Dr. McGrath now recommended radiation therapy.

As I listened to his voice, my mind began to race. Until then, I had thought I was fine. I knew that I had cancer—but it was "low-grade" and contained in the tumor that the doctors had excised. The muscles in my leg had been damaged, but I would rehabilitate them quickly. I was strong and healthy; I would recuperate in no time! Ten years earlier I had

had an appendectomy and was back to playing racquetball and even beat a younger friar only a couple of weeks later. I wondered if there had been an error in the pathology report. I couldn't believe that this aggressive cancer was within my body. But at the end of the conversation it seemed so final—his analysis was very definitive, the prognosis bleak.

As I hung up the phone, tears began to flow. In a moment all my plans had been shattered. I had known that I had a malignant tumor, but the words "low grade" and the doctors' opinion that surgery would suffice kept me from the realization that I had cancer. I said the word but did not understand the implications. Immediately after the operation the doctors said that they assumed they had gotten it all. I had thought I would be fine. I would direct my drive to rehabilitating my leg. I had already started planning how I could both teach my classes and exercise. It would be difficult, but I would meet the challenge; I was still in control and ready to do battle.

The news that the cancer was very aggressive, could easily metastasize and would require extensive treatment overwhelmed me. All of a sudden, my world had changed: a *thing* was controlling me. I couldn't make plans, a disease was disrupting my life, doctors were setting my course. I was no longer in control. I felt like a pawn. I wasn't even sure how to fight and overcome this enemy. And so I wept.

But as the tears dampened my pillow, an inner voice began to speak: "Your head is your main muscle.

Tears will not help; crying and feeling sorry for yourself will not remove the cancer." Making the best of a bad situation, allowing inner vision to determine my response rather than external events had always been my goal. I wanted to make the best of what was happening in my life, to deal as best I could with this cancer within me.

As I lay there, I thought about my friend Frank, who refuses to be defined by a handicap, who instead of sitting around feeling sorry for himself had decided to live. Preparing music for a liturgy, Frank and I had talked, practiced and played guitar together for weeks before I noticed that he had an artificial leg. One night after practice, he told his story. Years earlier, when he was a professional musician, driving home after a gig, his van was hit head-on by a drunk driver fleeing the police. The doctors had to amputate Frank's left leg. During his stay in the hospital, his fiancée called to break their engagement—she did not even visit—because she couldn't deal with what had happened. Frank told me how he cried for days over having lost not only his leg but also his love. One day he realized that he could spend the rest of his life feeling sorry for himself, or he could decide to live. He chose to live.

Frank (as well as Miss Manock and others) encouraged me to choose life, to act rather than react, to make the best of the situation. As the tears rolled down my cheeks, images of strength rose up within, showing me my choice. I wanted to deal with this cancer head-on and make the best of it, not feel sorry for myself.

I began to pray. The prayer that welled up within me then and in all the weeks and months that followed was not for healing, that the cancer be gone, that God perform some sort of miracle. Rather, I found myself praying for the strength to deal well with whatever happened and that I might find God in it all. Throughout my journey I would return often to that prayer. In fact, praying for the grace to deal well with cancer, with suffering, and to find God in the experience became my daily focus.

Different images of Francis presented themselves: Francis, lying on the ground, extremely ill, almost blind, unable to walk; Francis, too sick to visit his followers, writing to them about experiencing God through penance; Francis, brought low by grave illness, asking to be carried back to the Porziuncula to be with his brothers and bless them; Francis, too weak to travel to Assisi himself, inviting in song the mayor and bishop to reconcile their differences; Francis, near death, singing praise to God through all creation. Although he suffered much in the final years of his life, Francis was able to rise above his own pain and think of others, praise God, and even welcome "Sister Death."

Images of another more recent "Francis" also presented themselves. When the pain made sleeping at night impossible, I would try (not always successfully) to spend the time in prayer. I would hold my rosary and think about Joe Doino, a model of wholeness and holiness. Thoughts of him brought echoes of the homily preached at his funeral. One of his Franciscan classmates spoke about his many gifts and then revealed one that he had lacked—the gift of sleep. He wondered what Joe must have done all those hours, all those nights, throughout the years during which he suffered from insomnia. He believed that it was in those sleepless hours that Joe came to know the Good Shepherd, for he taught and preached not just as someone who knew a lot about God, but as someone who knew God intimately as Good Shepherd and friend.

Before my illness and surgery I was always able to sleep. It only took seconds for me to drift off, and I usually awoke well rested, even after a short night of sleep. But after surgery, because of the pain in my leg, I lacked the gift of sleep for the first time in my life. I found myself gazing upon the crucifix on my wall, praying that I might come to know the Lord like Joe—like Francis.

I longed to deepen my relationship with God but felt I didn't know how to pray, or at least how to pray well enough. The examples of mystics and holy people like Francis and Joe made my own prayer seem so inadequate. I tried to keep my heart from comparisons and to rest in the Lord as I am. But I brought to the Lord only my gnawing desire to know him and my fears and doubts about my prayer. It seemed so lacking then, but in retrospect, all of the searching, longing, gnawing and even speaking my fear and doubt was indeed prayer-full.

Why could I not see it as prayer then? Why can't we appreciate the fullness and blessing in the moment? Why do we so often not appreciate things until they're gone? Only with hindsight did that time of seemingly inadequate prayer become precious. Radiation treatments would soon make me feel so tired and sick that I could not pray. But I would come to realize that even then grace was at work.

I did not want radiation therapy, but my discussions with the doctors as well as some research convinced me that it was necessary. Thus, one month after surgery, I began the treatments. The radiation oncologist had studied the pathology report and discussed with me the aggressive nature of the cancer; he said that left untreated it could spread throughout my body within three to six months. He recommended maximum doses of radiation to the affected area of my leg in order to kill any remaining cancer cells.

He brought me into the set-up room. I was positioned on a table in the center of the room. People scurried about adjusting the table, lasers and monitors as I lay silent and listening. When the radiation field was determined, the points of the grid were tattooed onto my leg. The following Monday radiation treatments would begin.

That brief hour in the set-up room taught me much. I wanted to know all aspects of the treatment. I asked for a scientific explanation of how the radiation worked to control the cancer. In fact, I asked so many technical questions that the head of the department gave me two textbooks to take home. But my nonscientific learning that day was much more important. As I grew more uncomfortable and embarrassed hearing the oncologist instruct the women technicians to keep my genitals out of the radiation field, I sympathized with women who often are treated by male physicians. I studied the machines and listened to scientific explanations and wondered about people who might be terrified by them. I considered the astronomical costs and worried about people who lack health insurance and access to such treatments. As I tried to lie still in the pain and wondered about the course of the disease, I feared for people who face the ordeal of cancer alone or without faith.

That hour kindled my compassion. During the weeks that followed, the endless waiting for treatments, doctors, tests and lab work; the fatigue to the point of exhaustion; the daily nausea; the severe burn on my irradiated skin; and the splitting headache that developed during the last four weeks of treatment—all these drew me into deeper compassion for all patients undergoing painful treatments. Unfortunately, the nausea and constant headache prevented me from focusing, reading or doing much of anything—even praying. Not only did I feel sick, I felt frustrated that I was so unproductive and disappointed with myself for not praying. But I didn't have the energy. There was nothing to do but keep focused, endure and wait until I felt better. I pushed on and tried to make the best of it.

It was after radiation treatments that I first was called a *cancer survivor*.

People who have gone through chemotherapy or radiation treatments are commonly called cancer survivors, but I could not accept it and at times would even refuse to be identified as such. It seemed inadequate. My experience went beyond surviving: It had been an experience of grace. The physical and psychological pain and suffering; the inability to walk, jog, sit or sleep without pain; the weeks of radiation and hospital visits for tests and procedures; the worry of my family and the burdens on my Franciscan brothers were all difficult to endure. But there in it all was grace—abundant blessing! I identified with Francis among the lepers. Although at first it was difficult, painful and very bitter for him, it became a time of grace, a time of sweetness, a time when he experienced God's presence and abundant love more fully.

My journey with cancer has included many moments in which, as Francis put it after his time with the lepers, "what had seemed bitter to me was turned into sweetness of soul and body." Simple, ordinary things have affected me profoundly. Two stories that bespeak grace, two brief moments that image the bitter changed to sweetness of soul might help describe the experience *beyond* "survival."

When I was in pre-op, as I lay on the gurney talking with the anesthesiologist, one of the nurses told me that a member of my family was there to see me. I was puzzled. My family lives near Chicago. My sisters had wanted to come east to be with me, but I had talked them out of it. I wanted to be alone to rest and to pray. Moments later, Ron, one of my Franciscan brothers, entered my cubicle. He had come to be with me, to pray with me, to make sure that I was all right before surgery. In haste, we talked a bit, prayed briefly, and he blessed me as they prepared to wheel me off to surgery. He came to the recovery room to check on me again before he called my family and the friars. I don't remember his visit. I do remember opening my eyes later that evening in my hospital room to find Ron again standing over me. He wanted to make sure I was all right and told me not to worry about talking. He returned several times over the next few days, just to be there in case he could help in any way, always a gentle, caring presence, always respecting my need for rest, never expecting a response, and never overstaying his welcome. I felt blessed to have such a sensitive and generous brother. Throughout my ordeal I have become more aware of the blessing of brothers, a loving family and incredible friends. Cancer has brought me a new realization of many blessings. I was not just "surviving."

I slept fitfully during the night after my first surgery—it is never easy to sleep in a hospital with the staff bustling in the halls. By morning I was in much pain and very nauseated, but I tried to sleep. Sometime that morning, I opened my eyes and saw my friend Gerry. Knowing he lived an eight-hour drive away, I asked what he was doing there. He said

simply, "Padre, I needed to know you were all right."
He saw that I couldn't talk or even keep my eyes open
for long. He told me to rest. He sat in silence for a couple of hours next to my bed, and I held onto his hand
and rejoiced in the blessing of friends. Periodically, the
nausea overcame me. He faithfully assisted me and
offered water for my parched lips. No demands were
made by this friend, with whom I could be my ailing
self. His silent, faithful presence loudly bespoke love.
Cancer had brought us closer, as it would bring me
closer to many others, even to my God.

At times during my illness, my prayer intensified. It is hard to articulate, but I felt closer to Christ.
Life had become, as is often the case when we're faced
with death, more precious. It wasn't exactly a wake-up
call, since I had been trying to follow in the footsteps
of our Lord as a Franciscan, but it did deepen my spiritual experience. My illness has been for me a time of
grace.

Survivor captured nothing of these experiences for me; it merely indicated that I had gotten
through a physical crisis. It said nothing of grace. At
first I wasn't sure how to express it, but I had gone
beyond surviving.

One morning, as I lay on my bed trying to
pray, an image presented itself to me: *Brother Cancer!*
In that moment I understood how to speak about the
grace within the experience of cancer. The image
allowed me to name what I had found difficult to
describe, what I only had been able to express as some

of the positive aspects of being ill. Brother Cancer was the image I sought.

At last I could share my experience. Francis had taught me to seek God in all things; he had given me words and images from his own experience of God in the ordinary: Brother Sun and Sister Water, Brother Fire and Sister Earth, Brother Leper and Sister Death. Brother Cancer expressed the pain and the blessing, the illness as a time of grace, the bitter becoming sweet.

Images of Francis and echoes of his words toward the end of his life filled my head. Cancer had become my way of being led among the lepers. Though I had been searching for years, longing for intimacy with God, I felt I was just beginning. My encounter with the leper, cancer, began to change what seemed bitter into sweetness of soul and body. My encounter with Brother Cancer changed my life.

I was no mere survivor. I would no longer, could no longer be the same. I had encountered the leper; I had begun to see more clearly. I would try to learn from this as I continued to walk with that leper. I would continue to seek God and try to live intensely as I walked my path now with Brother Cancer.

Choosing the Colors

Francis Praying before the Crucifix at San Damiano.

Because the servant of the Most High
had no other teacher in these matters
except Christ,
His kindness visited him once more
in the sweetness of grace.

For one day when Francis went out to meditate in the fields, he walked near the church of San Damiano, which was threatening to collapse because of age. Impelled by the Spirit, he went inside to pray. Prostrate before an image of the Crucified, he was filled with no little consolation as he prayed. While his tear-filled eyes were gazing at the Lord's cross, he heard with his bodily ears a voice coming from that cross, telling him three times: "Francis, go and repair my house which, as you see, is all being destroyed."

Trembling, Francis was stunned at the sound of such an astonishing voice, since he was alone in the church; and as he absorbed the power of the divine words into his heart, he fell into an ecstasy of mind. At last, coming back to himself, he prepared himself to obey and pulled himself together to carry out the command of repairing the material church, although the principal intention of the words referred to that which Christ purchased with his own blood, as the Holy Spirit taught him and as he himself later disclosed to the brothers.

Then, after fortifying himself with the sign of the cross, he arose, and taking cloth to sell, he hurried off to a city called Foligno. There, after selling everything he had brought with him, even the horse he was riding, the successful merchant quickly returned with the price he had obtained. Returning to Assisi, he reverently entered the church he had received the command to repair. When he found the poor priest there, he showed him fitting reverence, offered him money for the repair of the church and for the use of the poor, and humbly requested that he be allowed to stay with him for a time. The priest agreed to his staying there but, out of fear of his parents, would not accept the money that the true scorner of wealth had thrown on a windowsill, valuing it no more than if it were dust.

—Bonaventure, *Legenda maior* II:1

The account of Francis praying before the crucifix in San Damiano presents a very human Francis: the capable apprentice who was doing well but searched for more, the young man who prayed to know God's will but was unsure of what he should do, the naive believer who responded to his call with great enthusiasm but was confused by the rejection by family and friends, the committed and generous servant who did much good but was unable to understand what it meant and where it was going. I can identify with that Francis—the young, impulsive, dramatic and committed lover of God who felt called and responded, but who would need years to sort out the meaning of that call and to come to know God more fully.

There were moments when Francis felt more alive or touched by God, pivotal experiences in which he clearly saw how he wanted to live. But his vision needed to develop. Over the years his vision would change and become more defined. Although he did not fully understand what he was to do, he had glimpsed Love, so he stayed with the journey. He continued his passionate quest to live more intensely, to respond out of love for the love with which he had been loved.

These experiences—praying before the crucifix, embracing the leper—drew Francis into the embrace of God. But he needed time to discover how to respond. At first, Francis responded very literally and began to repair the church of San Damiano with his own hands, begging stones from the townspeople. Later, Francis would feel called to serve the Lord in different ways: working with lepers, serving others as a lesser brother, praising God and preaching conversion.

As he continued to work with lepers and to pray, Francis's holiness—his commitment, intensity, inner joy and peace—attracted others. Bernard of Quintavalle wondered about Francis, a man who gave up everything yet wanted nothing, was rejected by his own father yet loved so passionately, was scorned for his work among the lepers yet sang joyful praise to God, owned no house yet felt so at home in the world, begged for food but proclaimed his riches, suffered much yet sang of his blessings. Through Francis, Bernard began to see. In Francis, Bernard found what he himself sought. Never had he known anyone to live with such intensity and passion, such peace and joy. And so, Bernard asked Francis if he could join him. Peter Catanii and Giles of Assisi soon followed—all of them attracted by the person of Francis, by a life of love that brought such peace.

The new brothers gave away what they had and began to do what Francis had been doing: working among the lepers, repairing abandoned churches, and singing the praises of God. Then one day, hearing the gospel proclaimed on the feast of St. Mathias, Francis suddenly understood more clearly how they should follow the Lord. The missionary discourse in the gospel—"take nothing for your journey"—

expressed the profound desires of his heart that he had been unable to articulate.

Even though Francis then "knew" what he and the brothers were called to do, he would spend years coming to understand that call more clearly. He wrote a Rule and continued to update and clarify it with the brothers for ten years. He continued to serve the needy and to work when he could. He even set off on a mission, hoping for martyrdom. Still, he struggled to know exactly what he was to do, how he was called to serve the Lord. He wondered if he should go off as a hermit to live a life of prayer or go among the people preaching the word of God. To help him decide, he sought the prayer and advice of Brother Sylvester and Lady Clare of Assisi.

Francis decided to remain among the people, but he would go apart for weeks at a time to pray, to a deserted place, a mountain retreat like La Verna, to be alone with God. High in the hills, apart from all distractions, Francis would fast and pray. There, years after his experience at San Damiano, of working with the lepers, there to pray and prepare to preach, there in the last years of his life, Francis would encounter Christ and come to know more fully God's abundant love in his life.

Those years speak to my heart. I have been living the Franciscan life of work, prayer and community for years. My head knows the words—*ministry, prayer, fraternity*—and can relate their meaning. But my heart still seeks a proper balance. I feel that I have only begun to pray. I know that I have done some good work in ministry, but my heart still yearns to know God intimately. I have studied theology and Francis's life, yet I am only beginning to understand. The fact that his life in God developed over years—that he continued to discern his vocation, struggled to know what he should do, spent months in prayer and fasting throughout the years before his mystical encounter with Christ on La Verna two years before his death—gives me hope and helps me to accept my own slowness.

Over the years Giotto's painting of Francis preaching to the birds has become more special to me. That image of Francis encompasses years of his life. No longer do I see an "instant" Francis, holy and perfect, but rather the years of gradual conversion. In the muted colors, open gesture and reverential posture, I now see depth, sensitivity and a profound experience of love. I see a Francis who knows his own humanity and with simple humility reaches out to the little ones. I see a Francis who, through his own human struggles and suffering, continued to love; a simple human being who knew he was loved despite his weakness and sin, and so was filled with gratitude; an ordinary person who, having tasted the mystery of love, lived passionately and loved intensely. This Francis encourages me to continue my journey and invites me to encounter God in others.

Giotto's image captures for me a Francis who grew through suffering, who struggled through the years to come to know and follow the Lord. That image speaks to my heart. Though Francis has taught me to find God in the ordinary, has helped me to name this cancer my brother, and offers me hope in my struggle, still I know that I have only begun the journey. I have been walking with this brother for several years now and realize that it is not enough to recognize cancer as brother; I need to continue to embrace this leper. Brother Cancer continues to teach me to open my eyes. At times I feel like a beginner, or like a resentful older brother who is too proud to listen, too stubborn to learn. At times I still don't see clearly enough, haven't learned enough, and wonder why it has taken me this long.

Throughout the fall semester, even when I felt sick and exhausted by the radiation treatments, I expected to be back teaching by the beginning of the spring semester in January. However, the wound in my leg never fully healed. To my chagrin I had to undergo another operation. I wanted the leg to heal, so I resigned myself to more surgery and another semester on medical leave.

I didn't really understand what was involved until the evening after surgery, the first time the doctors changed the dressing. I watched as they unwrapped the bandages. I gritted my teeth and tried not to yell. They had explained the procedure to me, but understanding the process didn't lessen the pain.

The dressing was changed twice a day, morning and evening. I got really good at dealing with pain.

And so, with a wound in my leg, I left the hospital some nine days later with doctor's orders to stay in my room for six weeks, as if I were still in the hospital. During that time, Brother Cancer taught me painful lessons in patience and humility.

The friars did many things for me. They took turns bringing meals to me in my room. Two of them even learned sterile technique to help me change the dressings. Alas, from being strong and independent I was reduced to weakness and dependence on my brothers. From being very active, I lived an imposed confinement. I wanted to make the best of the situation and tried to use much of my time in prayer and, at the urging of my brothers, to write about my experience with cancer.

Painfully, Brother Cancer forced me to focus on what was most essential in life. Obviously, I became grateful for things I had taken for granted: the ability to walk, to sleep without pain, to get my own food, and just to have a right leg that felt normal! I found myself remembering and praying for people who had loved me, had freely shared their lives with me, had been signs of God's love and grace in my life. Instead of focusing on being unable to walk or leave my room, I focused on the goodness of my brothers, the love of my family and so many friends, and so, despite frustrations and disappointment, I felt incredibly lucky and very blessed.

Instead of returning to teaching, I was again on medical leave. My life had changed in many ways.

It became punctuated by regular checkups. The doctors said that my type of cancer usually spreads first to the lungs, so they checked me every two months. The tests continued uneventfully, and I continued to regain strength. I longed to return to jogging and promised myself that when I *could* run I *would* run—no matter what the weather—just because I could do it. As soon as I could begin exercising, I did so with a passion. I grew stronger, and the following fall I returned to the classroom full time, grateful because I love teaching.

I knew that Brother Cancer had taught me much. But, as often occurs in such a relationship, I was not always ready to listen, learn or grow through suffering with my brother. As I returned to teaching, I wondered if I could live the new vision that my walk with Brother Cancer had given me. Everything was the same, yet nothing was the same. I directed all my energies to my ministry, and I wondered if I could sustain the intensity. People told me I looked great. Outward appearances suggested that I now walked alone, without Brother Cancer.

As I grew stronger, I feared that I might lose focus on what is essential and be caught up in the superficial concerns of daily routine and commitments. As I began to walk more quickly and less painfully, I sensed the danger in forgetting or paying less attention to my former companion. I feared the loss of his graced presence. I wanted to continue living as when I was "led among the lepers." I did not want to be ill, but I did not want to be simply or superficially healthy. I did not want to be just a survivor, to return to my regular tasks and hectic schedule, however exciting and fulfilling.

My first full day of teaching, although it was six months after my second operation and followed months of walking and exercise, resulted in swelling and pain in my bad leg. Nonetheless, I was so excited to be back teaching that I found it easy to see beyond the pain. I reminded myself of when I couldn't even get out of bed or could only hobble around my room. I remembered the pain following both surgeries. Brother Cancer had taught me that pain is relative. One of the sisters at the motherhouse thought I shouldn't kneel during mass because she had seen me wince. I told her that I was happy to be *able* to kneel again, and so the pain was inconsequential. It didn't convince her, but I didn't stop kneeling either.

Not only had Brother Cancer taught me about suffering, he had introduced me to others who suffered more than I and reminded me to be grateful. The day I returned to full-time teaching, I wanted to celebrate new beginnings, so on my way to my office I visited with a colleague who has always been a model for me. Al, a retired biology professor and renaissance man, taught an introductory humanities course. I wanted to share with him my excitement about being back but also find out how he was doing.

For years, Al has suffered severely from rheumatoid arthritis. That morning he greeted me as always, with great joy, enthusiasm, respect and concern. We talked about my health and prognosis, his continuing struggle with pain and treatments, about our courses and our experiences during the summer. Not then, not ever, have I heard him utter a word of complaint or self-pity. Al drinks deeply from the well of life and inspires me. A man of faith, a person of vision, a teacher in and out of the classroom, Al chooses life. Though he admits his limitations, he does not allow arthritis to define him; though constantly in pain, he sees the good; though understandably tempted to self-absorption, he focuses on others and opens himself to life. As I moved through the day, I thought of Al and my own pain ebbed. I prayed for the grace to live in faith with vision, always to choose life.

Only later could I admit that the return to teaching was difficult. Besides the constant pain in my leg, I tired quickly. I struggled to be patient with my body or "Brother Ass," as Francis called his. I wanted to return full force to everything that I had done before, but I had to learn further lessons in patience. The year was indeed good, not despite but through the pain and struggles.

I was thrilled to be back teaching, but because of Brother Cancer's lessons, I longed for a sabbatical. Since I was the only member of the theology department who had not had a sabbatical, I applied and was approved for one to begin the following September.

In my letter I had written: "My bout with cancer has only inflamed my desire to do *what is mine to do.*"

Francis's biographers tell us that before he died, he told the brothers, "I have done what is mine to do, may Christ teach you what is yours to do." Brother Cancer had helped me to hear that challenge. I felt a need to do what was mine to do—some research and writing. I planned to spend my sabbatical in Rome, at the Historical Institute of the Capuchins. As my departure date drew near, I grew more excited. Dr. McGrath had told me that I could be monitored in Italy as well as in the States, and he referred me to two doctors that he knew from international conferences. I headed out to have my last checkup with him and to pick up letters of introduction for the Italian physicians. But just five days before my departure, my plans changed again.

After studying my x-ray, Dr. McGrath told me that he saw something that didn't look right. I viewed it with him, and he pointed out the irregularity, but my untrained eye could barely perceive anything. Knowing that I planned to leave for Italy within a week, he scheduled me for a CT scan that afternoon. Unfortunately, it confirmed that there was a mass on my right lung, so we scheduled a biopsy for the following week. I would have to postpone my departure for a least a couple of weeks.

The biopsy took less than an hour. The more difficult part followed—waiting. The biopsy was on the Friday before Labor Day weekend; no one would even begin the analysis before the following Tuesday.

During the ninety-minute drive home to the university, I kept repeating, "Lord, I don't want this." I felt frustrated and disappointed. I was not focused on the cancer per se, but on my shattered hopes and plans. I had been so excited about going to Rome, getting away to do research and seeing my friends in Italy.

Those days of waiting were terrible. My whole life was on hold. My family and friends kept calling, but I had no news. Even if the news were bad, I would have preferred to know so that I could get on with living. Finally, late on Wednesday afternoon, I got a call from Dr. McGrath—the news was not good. The results indicated malignancy. The tumor would have to be excised as soon as possible. My departure would need to be postponed a couple of months.

It was not easy to readjust my focus. I had been excited about my sabbatical, about leaving for Rome, about the change and possibilities. Classes had started, and everyone at the university was busy with the new school year. I felt isolated and alone. I didn't want to overreact; I didn't want to bring anyone down. I tried to find whatever good I could. I prayed a lot—albeit distractedly. I found myself praying that I would deal well with whatever happened. I busied myself with all the last-minute changes. I postponed my ticket and notified my friends in Rome. I made an appointment to meet with the thoracic surgeon. I set my sights on making the best of things. I thought about the graces that I had experienced along the difficult walk with Brother Cancer. I lived in hope, hope that included going to Rome…eventually.

Two days later I again drove myself to the hospital. Before meeting with the surgeon, Dr. Urschel, I had to take a battery of tests. I was surprised at how quickly I moved through the different offices and labs. A number of the people taking information and performing tests on me, upon seeing the name of my surgeon, commented that he was excellent. Even before meeting Dr. Urschel, I was calm and confident about the upcoming surgery, and my initial meeting with him, as well as all our subsequent interactions, confirmed this. Everything about him convinced me that he was capable, competent and caring. And so, even amid the bad news, I felt lucky and blessed in some sense.

Dr. Urschel described a relatively simple operation, but it ended up being more extensive than planned. Given the original description of the surgery, I was surprised at the extent of the pain when I awoke—that is, until I heard what actually had been done to me.

It hurt to move, and it hurt just to lie in bed. I couldn't even push myself up in bed without excruciating pain. I quickly realized how difficult it is to do anything without using the muscles in your chest. I couldn't lift anything. I couldn't even get in or out of bed without assistance for the first two weeks after surgery. I had thought it was a good sign that I had been admitted to the hospital on the feast of the Exaltation of the Holy Cross and released three days later on the feast of the Stigmata of St. Francis. I joked with the friar who drove me home about being only one-fifth ready to celebrate it because I had only one of the five wounds. But I quickly changed the conversation to something more serious because I couldn't laugh. I couldn't laugh, sneeze, cough or even move without pain—so much pain that I didn't notice the pain in my leg for days!

My doctors recommended no further treatments but suggested that I see an oncologist. I returned to Dr. Lutz, whom I had seen a year before, a good and faith-filled man. We spoke about my medical history, Franciscans and Jesuits, and of course, the prognosis and recommended treatment. The good news: no chemotherapy. The bad news: chemotherapy would probably not prevent the cancer's spread. Dr. Lutz spoke about hope and tried to give me a reason to want to fight and keep living. I told him of my experience of cancer as a grace, my fear that I would predecease my mother, about my faith, St. Francis and Brother Cancer.

Once again, Brother Cancer would speak to me about patience, about pain being relative, and about my own fragility and finitude. He would impose a long time of rest, reflection, healing and prayer. Here again, amid even greater pain, I would know many blessings. One of those blessings was time with my sister.

My sister Patti came and stayed at the friary to help me during the first week of recuperation. Initially I had resisted her offer to come; I did not want to be a burden to her or to anyone. Afterward I was most grateful. I depended on her. Because of the pain, I needed help getting in and out of bed, and she was there to help me. The pain intensified if I didn't change positions, so she would get up at two or three in the morning to help me into a chair, and then she'd go back to bed. Patti had trouble getting back to sleep in the middle of the night, but she never complained. She appeared faithfully in the middle of the night and again in the early morning—always cheerful and ready to serve. I was grateful for her incredible goodness to me, but even more so for the gift of time we had together.

Both of us have led busy lives. That week it was as if time had stopped. Once I was helped to my feet, I could walk—slowly and for short distances. But walk we did, increasing our journey each day. We walked together along the trail by the river, amid the fall foliage. We walked in the morning and again in the afternoon. I would take her arm and slowly we would set off on our path. Those moments remain precious. I held her arm; she touched my heart. We talked about the family and growing up; our hopes, faith and doubts; about death and life; about what is essential; about sharing love. We had always been friends; we had spent a lot of time together over the years traveling back and forth to high school together, working in the garden and building rock walls.

In the book given to Patti on her fiftieth birthday I had written:

> You have shown your love for me in countless ways. Over the years I have seen you give of your very self again and again. One recent example that immediately comes to mind is the time that you helped me care for the wound in my leg. I know that you don't deal well or easily with some of these messy medical things. In fact, I hesitated to let you assist me since I feared you might faint. But your determination to help me in my pain, your willingness to put aside your own revulsion because I needed assistance, again became love writ large and friendship embodied so that I could not but feel much, much loved.

Brother Cancer had given me another gift. My illness created sacred space in which Patti and I became even closer.

I reluctantly took a low dose of pain medication for the first few days. I hate taking any type of medication, and, as is always the case for me with anesthesia or pain medication, I got sick. My sister entered into my painful, awkward, unpleasant and embarrassing situations and loved me. She walked with me, and her love became incarnate. I could see Francis walking among the lepers, entering into their pain and sorrow, sharing mundane moments, bringing a reverence even to awkward and unpleasant situations—love transforming each encounter. Patti's love transformed those days into extraordinary, sacred time.

Other blessings would follow. About two months later, as soon as I was strong enough to travel, I left for my sabbatical in Rome, as originally planned. My friend Pietro, one of the Capuchins at the *Istituto*, met me at the airport. He has accompanied me from afar along this cancer journey—e-mails, phone calls, deep concern and constant prayer. His concern about my health and his readiness to help me continued through those months.

While in Rome I had the chance to visit Assisi and La Verna often. I visited friends in Fermo, Sorrento, Florence, Bologna and Venice. It was not the places but the people who refreshed my soul, spoke to me of God, and were vehicles of grace. I was invited to preach and give conferences at various places, and each experience brought blessings. Every time I have tried to share my journey with Brother Cancer and my experience of God, the exchange has been grace-filled for me.

My encounter with Brother Cancer has been like Francis's experience of hearing the gospel proclaimed on the feast of St. Mathias, when he suddenly saw how he was called to follow the Lord. I believe that I now see this Franciscan journey, this life as a lesser brother that I began years ago, more clearly.

Things are not perfectly clear, nor have I finished the journey. Even St. Francis needed time to focus his vision and to understand God's presence and call in his life. I have become more patient with myself, with the length of the journey, with my lingering blindness. And so I continue. I hope that in walking further with Brother Cancer I might see what is essential, understand my call to follow the Lord and live the gospel more truly, become a more faithful follower of Francis. I hope that I can incorporate what I have learned from Brother Cancer. I hope that I can live—or paint—with more determination, passion and intensity.

Painting a Portrait

Francis Receiving the Stigmata.

Two years before he returned his spirit to heaven,
after a variety of many labors,
he was led by divine providence
to a high place apart called Mount La Verna.
When according to his usual custom
he had begun to fast there for forty days
in honor of St. Michael the Archangel,
he experienced more abundantly than usual
an overflow of the sweetness of heavenly contemplation,
was on fire with an ever intense flame of heavenly desires,
and began to be aware more fully of the gifts of heavenly entries....

With the seraphic ardor of desires,
therefore,
he was being borne aloft into God;
and by compassionate sweetness
he was being transformed into Him
Who chose to be crucified out of
the excess of His love.

On a certain morning about the feast of the Exaltation of the Cross, while Francis was praying on the mountainside, he saw a Seraph having six wings, fiery as well as brilliant, descend from the grandeur of heaven. And when in swift flight, it had arrived at a spot in the air near the man of God, there appeared between the wings the likeness of a man crucified, with his hands and feet extended in the form of a cross and fastened to a cross. Two of the wings were raised above his head, two were extended for flight, and two covered his whole body. Seeing this, he was overwhelmed and his heart was flooded with a mixture of joy and sorrow. He rejoiced at the gracious way Christ looked upon him under the appearance of the Seraph, but the fact that He was fastened to a cross pierced his soul with a sword of compassionate sorrow.

He marveled exceedingly
at the sight of so unfathomable a vision,
knowing that the weakness of Christ's passion
was in no way compatible
with the immortality of the seraphic spirit.
Eventually he understood from this,
through the Lord revealing it,
that divine providence had shown him a vision of this sort so that,
the friend of Christ might learn in advance
that he was to be totally transformed
into the likeness of Christ crucified,
not by the martyrdom of his flesh,
but by the enkindling of his soul.

As the vision was disappearing,
it left in his heart a marvelous fire
and imprinted in his flesh a likeness of signs
no less marvelous.

For immediately the marks of nails began to appear in his hands and feet just as he had seen a little before in the figure of the man crucified. His hands and feet seemed to be pierced through the center by nails, with the heads of the nails appearing on the inner side of the hands and the upper side of the feet and their points on the opposite sides. The heads of the nails in his hands and his feet were round and black; their points were oblong and bent as if driven back with a hammer, and they emerged from the flesh and stuck out beyond it. Also his right side, as if pierced with a lance, was marked with a red wound from which his sacred blood often flowed, moistening his tunic and underwear....

After true love of Christ
transformed the lover into his image,
when the forty days were over that he spent in solitude
as he had desired,
and the feast of St. Michael the Archangel
had also arrived,
the angelic man Francis
came down from the mountain, bearing with him
the likeness of the Crucified,
depicted not on tablets of stone or on panels of wood
carved by hand,
but engraved on parts of his flesh
by the finger of the living God.
—Bonaventure, *Legenda maior*, XIII:1–3, 5

*T*hough most people encounter Francis at Assisi, La Verna reveals the heart of Francis's experience, vision and life. The stigmata represent not an isolated moment but the culmination of a lifelong journey, and offer a key to understanding him at a more profound level.

Francis often sought out mountain retreats for solitude and prayer, as he did in the fall of 1224 at La Verna. He probably could not explain *symbol* in abstract theological terms, but he understood its meaning at his depths, knew its power in his bones. He experienced the transcendent in and through reality. For years, Francis had been transfixed by Jesus Christ, Word of God, born in Bethlehem, crucified on the cross. In gazing upon the Christ, he could see, taste and feel the love of God.

Francis's embrace of God did not begin at La Verna. He had already experienced God's love in his life. Francis experienced God's love through encounter with others, serving the poor, giving of himself, offering peace, admitting his sin. He encountered God in the ordinary, sought God in the concrete, saw God revealed in all of creation. Francis would try to draw others into the experience of God's love through the concrete. On Christmas Eve at Greccio, one year before his experience on Mount La Verna, Francis had a crèche constructed where mass would be celebrated so that people could *see* the love of God incarnate in the Babe of Bethlehem.

Where and how did Francis experience this love of God? In the love of his parents, giving alms to the poor, the embrace of the leper, caring for the sick? Certainly his experience at La Verna was the deepening of an already profound experience of God's love, one tied intimately to Christ crucified as the revelation of this love. His own suffering became a grace for him because it drew him more deeply into the suffering of Christ, the revelation of God's love.

In Christ crucified, Francis saw the humility of God. God's love so overwhelmed Francis that he spoke of God's "humble sublimity and sublime humility." In his second account of the life of Francis, Thomas of Celano speaks about Francis's devotion to the love of God, attributing a beautiful Latin phrase to him: *Eius qui nos multum amavit, multum est amor amandus* (2 Cel 196). Perhaps it is too polished to have originated with Francis, but it does sum up his vision: "The love of him who loved us much is much to be loved." This is quintessential *Francis*. He knew, experienced, tasted the love of God and proclaimed it with his very being. All of his life—serving lepers, rebuilding churches, praising God and preaching penance, working with others while refusing dominion over them, living in poverty in order to share the gifts of creation, writing and rewriting a Rule with his brothers, lying naked on the bare ground to welcome Sister

Death—proclaimed this vision: "We should love intensely the love of him who loved us so intensely."

At La Verna, Francis loved even more intensely the love of God who first loved him so intensely. But this journey of love had begun years earlier at Assisi, when he was a beloved son playing in the piazza, helping his parents and dreaming of glory; a respected friend leading celebrations, seeking the glory of knighthood, then living among lepers and begging stones to repair churches; a cherished brother living the gospel, preaching volumes without words, loving as a mother would her child. At La Verna we more clearly see the vision that all along gave form to his life and shape to his "painting."

Brother Cancer points toward La Verna. He has invited me to see what has given shape to my own painting. Although I am not yet ready or able to ascend the heights of La Verna, Brother Cancer has brought me to the plains below, has invited me to gaze upward and to see Francis. Brother Cancer has helped me to begin the ascent, to gain some perspective in looking back over my life; he has challenged me to move forward and to continue the uphill struggle.

The question of how I have found peace with cancer has also brought me to La Verna. It has led me to look more clearly at my life and has challenged me to embrace Brother Cancer more fully and to live more intensely. Hindsight has brought forth some of the critical moments in my life; Brother Cancer has clarified my vision.

I have been much blessed in my life—not only in the love I have received, but also in being called and drawn into the Franciscan vision. I have been blessed in coming to know Francis—not only by studying his writings and the early sources, but also through the Franciscans I have met and especially some of the friars with whom I have lived. I do not mean to suggest that everyone literally should become a Franciscan. But I do believe that Francis speaks to everyone's deepest longing precisely because he shows how we can experience God in the ordinary, coming to know God through Christ, embracing the cross as gift, giving of self and receiving life.

I am very blessed. Brother Cancer has brought my loving family and me even closer; I have felt the power of countless prayers (especially those of my Franciscan family and friends, including many Poor Clares and Capuchin nuns whom I have never met). He has called me to live more intensely, to live more fully in Christ—which is what I am supposed to be about as a Christian and as a Franciscan. How can I say Brother Cancer is evil, sad or awful?

At the same time, I need to say that I feel freer to embrace this cancer than those who have families. I don't know how I would react if I had children. I assume that cancer is much more difficult for someone like my friend Becky, who has two small children. She doesn't deny the pain—the nausea, fatigue, the psychological and physical suffering. She has talked with me about her fear of leaving behind her husband Mark and their two children, her concern about *their* suffering. Yet Becky has talked about some of the blessings of cancer, about the deeper intimacy that she, her husband and their two young boys share.

In walking with Brother Cancer I have experienced the mystery of the cross or what Francis called the blessing of penance. Unfortunately, I am not always attentive to the call, not always able or willing to embrace the cross, not always ready to serve out of the love wherein we experience the gift of life and promise of resurrection. Brother Cancer has given me moments in which I can glimpse the meaning of resurrection amid tears of joy, a sign of our own resurrection experiences. Those moments offer us a taste of the resurrection and help us to understand and to believe that in dying to self we find life. Perhaps what I am trying to say will become clear if I share an incident that occurred a few months after my second operation.

Long before I began my journey with cancer, I had agreed to give a retreat for priests in the diocese of Oakland. Although my leg ached, I was back at work and wanted to keep my commitment, so I flew to Oakland for the week-long retreat. My schedule included three conferences a day as well as the homily during mass. Every moment was consumed with trying to prepare talks and meeting with the priests who wanted to talk with me between conferences. I found no time to fit in exercise to help the circulation in my leg, and it ached constantly. I began to wonder if I had erred in not canceling the retreat.

When the pain became acute, I reminded myself of what one of my Franciscan brothers had told me when I first considered honoring the commitment. Regis, a good theologian and excellent preacher who himself had given many retreats to diocesan priests, simply said: "They very much need spiritual nourishment, and you can give that." His words had encouraged me both to accept the invitation initially and then later to fulfill my commitment. Thus, I threw myself wholeheartedly into the retreat. I wanted to share my faith, my experience of God's love and goodness in my life. I tried hard to forget the pain. It was a difficult struggle—until the fifth day, until the communal celebration of the sacrament of reconciliation, until a conversation I will always remember.

It had been a long day. For a couple of hours that evening I had been having private talks with some of the retreatants. I was very tired and my leg ached. I longed to return to my room, but I tried to listen attentively as one of the priests began to speak with me. His voice was strong, his face serious, his tone sad. He had not wanted to make the retreat, he began. He was there only because the bishop insisted. He had lost all enthusiasm for his priestly ministry, his desire to be a priest and to celebrate the sacraments. Somewhere along the way, he had lost his passion and vision. With grateful but heavy heart, I listened as he described his life and ministry. His openness, his honesty and humility, and his willingness to be vulnerable touched me deeply. The ache I felt for him in my heart left me unprepared for what followed.

As he continued, his voice faltered and his eyes filled with tears. He said that my words, my faith and my enthusiasm had pierced his heart and rekindled in him the desire to return to the Lord, to minister as a priest, to grow closer to God and experience God's love more fully. He spoke about his profound gratitude for the blessings he had received. As he continued to speak about his change of heart, with the tears now rolling down his cheeks, as he took my hands into his and said thank you, I too began to cry.

Those tears of joy that we shared spoke to me of the presence of grace, God's healing love at work in the sacrament and our encounter. In that moment the ache in my leg melted away. All the pain I had felt that week became a small price to pay to witness the presence of God's healing love within the sacrament of reconciliation. I too was grateful that God had been able to use me, that I had been a vehicle of grace. Those tears of joy reminded me that in giving we receive, in dying to self we find life. Amid our tears of joy, we tasted the promise of resurrection.

If only we were always attentive to God's call, always ready to give and to serve and so become more aware of the blessing of God and the life that comes through dying to our own selfishness. In walking with Brother Cancer, I have been offered more of these possibilities, and so the journey has been blessed. But

I need to remain open to God's call, ever more ready and willing to embrace the cross, less concerned about my own physical state—all symbolized by "my" tree.

I found my tree in the fall, after the operation to remove the tumor in my chest. By then I no longer felt very good about myself physically. Earlier in my life, although I was never completely satisfied, I had felt good about myself, but after the operations and treatments I had lost that positive sense of self. *I* knew that my leg and chest were disfigured, even if it was not immediately apparent to others. I lived with pain reminding me that my body was not well. I worked hard to get back into shape. I learned to look beyond the pain and be grateful for how much it had lessened. But I didn't feel my own beauty. I was—I fear I still am—caught up in our culture's idea of beauty as physical, judging myself and others on the superficial level of appearances.

One sunny fall day, just after the feast of St. Francis, I found a tree—*my* tree—along the footpath by the river. After the last operation, what had been my regular jogging route had become my walking path. I moved slowly, thinking and praying, listening to the rustling of leaves, drinking in the glorious colors of fall, following the currents and eddies of the glistening water, marveling at the beauty of creation all about me. I looked up and, caught by surprise, stopped in my tracks. There before me stood a tree that I had never noticed, a tree that now drew me. There in the midst of magnificence and majesty, bent and broken in the shadow of others, a misshapen tree spoke my name. I stood and stared. My eyes followed its mangled and rotting trunk, which leaned toward the river. The tree's scars revealed its suffering.

I began to identify with that misshapen and ailing tree. I began to reflect on my own body image—scarred and disfigured—but I was also drawn to the new life that surged forth from that trunk. New branches, straight and tall, alive and flourishing, stretched toward the sun. I began to view that tree, *my* tree, as a symbol of new life, as a call for me to grow and develop, to reach toward the Son, to find and to nurture the new life that surged within a misshapen and cancerous body.

I returned the next day with camera in hand, took shots from various angles, and finished a roll of film. I wanted to capture the image of my tree before it shed its leaves; I wanted to gaze upon my tree in my room, my symbol of new life out of suffering, my call to live more intensely. My tree symbolizes how I hope to walk with Brother Cancer, how I hope, through grace, that my scarred and ailing body might live more intensely and grow toward the Son. My tree symbolizes living with faith, living in love, living right up to the moment of greeting Sister Death. And so I gaze upon my tree: picture, symbol, call.

Transforming Textures

Francis Celebrating Christmas at Greccio.

It happened, three years prior to his death, that he decided to celebrate at the town of Greccio the memory of birth of the Child Jesus with the greatest possible solemnity, in order to arouse devotion. So that this would not be considered a type of novelty, he petitioned for and obtained permission from the Supreme Pontiff.

He had a manger prepared,
hay carried in and an ox and an ass led to the spot.
The brethren are summoned,
the people arrive,
the forest amplifies with their cries,
and that venerable night is rendered
brilliant and solemn
by a multitude of bright lights
and by resonant and harmonious hymns of praise.

The man of God stands before the manger,
filled with piety,
bathed in tears and overcome with joy.
A solemn Mass is celebrated over the manger,
with Francis, a levite of Christ, chanting the holy Gospel.

Then he preaches to the people standing around him
about the birth of the poor King,
whom, whenever he means to call him,
he called in his tender love,
the Babe from Bethlehem.

A certain virtuous and truthful knight,
Sir John of Greccio,
who had abandoned worldly military activity out of love of Christ
and had become an intimate friend of the man of God,
claimed that he saw a beautiful little child asleep in that manger
whom the blessed father Francis embraced in both of his arms
and seemed to wake it from sleep.

Not only does the holiness of the witness
make credible
the vision of the devout knight,
but also the truth it expresses
proves its validity
and the subsequent miracles confirm it.

For Francis's example,
when considered by the world
is capable of arousing
the hearts of those who are sluggish in the faith of Christ.
—Bonaventure, *Legenda maior* X:7

$\mathcal{B}$onaventure's narration of the story of St. Francis setting up the first Nativity crèche speaks to me of miracles and of my journey with cancer. In his retelling of that Christmas celebration at Greccio in 1223, Bonaventure captures the heart of the story in his description of the miracle witnessed by Sir John of Greccio, the heart of my cancer journey and an image of the miracle for which I pray.

For people of faith, cancer, more than other diseases, raises the question of miracles. I must admit with some embarrassment that I am confused about miracles. But soon after the doctors diagnosed my cancer, the question began to confront me.

Friends here in the States wanted to take me to Lourdes; friends in Italy to the shrine of Padre Pio—someplace where I would be cured. Countless others have been besieging the heavens, many with a single goal: a miracle, that I be healed, that God remove this cancer from me.

Bonaventure records various miracles, including healings, which have been attributed to St. Francis. These accounts of miracles can largely be explained in terms of thirteenth-century hagiography. But how do we explain the miracles in our world today? My own wondering about miracles finds expression in Bonaventure's sketch of the miracle at Greccio.

Bonaventure relates that John of Greccio, a holy man and close friend of Francis, saw a child lying in the manger and saw Francis embrace it. We could focus on the miracle of Greccio as an apparition, a vision seen by Sir John. But the texts speak more profoundly of the miracle wrought by the presence of Francis, and of the Child of Bethlehem brought to life within the hearts of people through the life and love of Francis.

That, for me, is the miracle. We too often look at miracles only as extraordinary physical acts. But to expect or to pray for physical change restricts miracles to a superficial level. The important miracles are the changes in people's hearts.

Francis's approach to his own illness and suffering helps me in my struggle with cancer and my understanding of miracles. Toward the end of his life, besides other infirmities that prevented him from moving around freely, he suffered from an eye disease that left him almost totally blind. His companions brought him to a hermitage at Fonte Colombo for treatment. The doctor, following the normal treatment in those days, prepared to cauterize Francis's eyes. But even though he was almost blind, he did not pray that his sight be restored. Rather, as the doctor readied to apply the poker, Francis prayed that Brother Fire might be gentle with him.

Not surprisingly, we do not find Francis praying for a miraculous healing for himself. Even though many stories attest that Francis healed the blindness of others, he prayed that Brother Fire be gentle. He prayed that he would be able to endure the inevitable. Initially reluctant to seek medical assistance for himself, Francis followed the counsel of his brothers and submitted himself to the doctor. He willingly endured the suffering caused by his illnesses and treatments. Bonaventure states that Francis was not concerned about his physical sight but only about being able to see God. Whatever happened in his life, Francis sought God in the experience—and this is paradigmatic for me. In the ordinary, in the physical, in his day-to-day experience, Francis would see God, could taste God and so celebrated God.

In his *Testament*, looking back over his life, remembering God's action and the important moments in his life, Francis mentions nothing of the miraculous—that is, in the sense of supernatural physical intervention. Francis does not even mention the stigmata, his mystical experience on Mount La Verna when, through his intense identification with Christ crucified, the wounds of Christ were imprinted on his body. Rather, Francis speaks about the miracle of being led among the lepers, of experiencing God in the ordinary, of the work of grace and the transformation of bitter into sweet. Francis lived among the lepers and came to see differently. Francis embraced what was difficult and painful in his life and found God there. This is quintessential Francis! This Francis informs my prayer and remains my model.

I don't believe in a God who toys with human beings or is manipulated by our prayers into changing the course of events. Yet, even though I most often pray that others and I will deal well with illness and find God in the pain, when I see people suffering, at times my prayer falls into a plea that they be healed. Whenever I think of Becky and the progression of her cancer, when I think of her two young children and devoted husband, when I remember our tears and words of hope, I find it difficult not to pray that she be healed.

I have met so many people in pain. Brother Cancer has introduced me to many of those with whom he walks, but my heart especially pains for the young who suffer. I do not expect a miracle for myself, at least in the sense that my cancer may be healed or removed. My own prayer has never been that my cancer be gone. That has never surged up spontaneously within me. On a conscious, reflective level, I do not want to pray like that, would not allow myself to pray for a miracle—that is, for *me*. Yet, while I cannot pray that my cancer may be healed, I can and do pray that others will be healed. This needs explanation, and it revolves around my understanding of prayer.

I do believe in the power of prayer. I pray each day and take prayer very seriously. When I promise to pray for someone, I try to remain faithful to that commitment. But even as I profess my belief in prayer, I admit that some of its power might be explained scientifically. I believe that there are different forms and levels of energy affecting us that we do not yet understand. I believe that in the future we will learn more, not only about the mind/body relationship but also about the spirit/body relationship. We might then be able to explain the power of prayer, in part, through an understanding of the relationship between energy and matter or spirit and matter.

But even if the connections cannot be fully explained now, I believe in the positive effect that both presence and prayer can have on people. I experienced the power of love and prayer accompanying me through operations and treatments. Ever since the metastasis of my cancer, when the doctors told me that there was a 95 percent chance that it would continue to spread in my body, every time I go for a check-up and the doctors do not find anything, I sense they are surprised, and I wonder again about the power of prayer. Over these months I have joked with people about "running on prayer." I wonder if all these prayers are not affecting my body positively, giving me not only more courage but also more energy to inhibit cancer and to nurture growth. So I pray—not for things but for people, not for cures but for blessings. I am most comfortable praying for others, but I also pray for myself—for openness to God, for the courage to respond to God's love. Yet there is a side to this mind/body relationship that haunts me.

If there is a mind/body relationship, if our belief and prayer can affect us, what about negative events in our lives? There is a doctor who claims that cancer is psychosomatic, that all cancer patients unconsciously *need* to have cancer. I have wondered if I need to have cancer, and that troubles me. Some illnesses *are* psychosomatic, and some people *might* need to have cancer. But I believe those are rare cases.

We don't have complete control over our physical well-being, conscious or unconscious. At times things just go wrong within the incredibly complex human body with all its interrelated organs and systems. Maybe some day we will know more about the causes of cancer—whether it is caused more by genetics or environment. Whatever causes it, something goes wrong within the body. Cells grow abnormally and damage the living system.

I know this in my head, but it doesn't erase the nagging doubt. Do I *need* to have cancer? Do I need it to distinguish myself, to excuse other inadequacies? My head tells me that no cancer patient should have to suffer the additional burden of feeling responsible for his or her illness. But it takes a long time to inform one's gut. So I pray that I not need my cancer but that I accept it, that I not view myself through the eyes of others but through the eyes of God, that I not try to be great but genuine, not well-liked but humble.

To return to my "running on prayer" and my belief in the power of prayer, even though I am not praying for a miracle, I know that many of those praying for me are praying for a cure, interceding on my behalf to Padre Pio or other saints, asking for a miracle. A Franciscan sister at Rome gave me a relic of

Padre Pio; my friend Pietro wanted to take me on pilgrimage to San Giovanni Rotondo, Padre Pio's shrine. I am not sure how to integrate these things into my life, but they are important and have had a real effect on me. And that brings me to my encounter with Padre Guglielmo.

Two Capuchins, whom I met in Rome, introduced me to a holy friar from their province with a reputation for miraculous cures. On our way to a dinner engagement, one of them, Alfredo, insisted that we visit a church in Faenza where there was a "miraculous crucifix." As we moved toward the side chapel where the crucifix hung, he began to speak about Padre Guglielmo, an elderly Capuchin priest known for his holiness who spent most of his day in the church. After celebrating mass early in the morning, he stayed to hear confessions and pray with people.

There was a line of people waiting to see Padre Guglielmo, and Alfredo told us about two incidents, which he admitted he could not explain or understand: two of his acquaintances who had had terminal cancer had been cured after Padre Guglielmo prayed with them. He then went over to Padre Guglielmo.

As Alfredo spoke with him, I prayed before the crucifix. When I looked up, Padre Guglielmo was standing before me. It was a graced moment, and I felt blessed to meet him. My heart filled with gratitude as silence befell me. I looked up into his eyes that beamed with joy and waited for him to speak. To my surprise, Padre Guglielmo told me how good it was to meet me. True humility is a mark of holiness, and Padre Guglielmo's humble manner confirmed his holiness for me. We spoke for a time, and then he took my hands and began to pray. My intellect might have told me that I should pray for my own cure, but my heart would not allow me. As this holy man prayed, I held my friends who also had cancer in prayer and asked that they be cured. For myself, I prayed that I might be open and deal well with whatever lay ahead, and that I might find God through this journey. I felt peace, a very powerful, even strange sense of peace, as if something deep inside me had been touched or changed.

I still haven't digested that encounter with Padre Guglielmo. I know that I felt a sense of awe and respect, an overwhelming sense of the presence of God, and an abiding peace deep within me. I did not know what Alfredo had said to him; I assumed he had told him that I had cancer and asked him to pray with me. Later I would learn from Alfredo that he had simply said that he had a friend, a friar from the United States, whom he wanted to introduce.

Long have I wondered about my encounter with Padre Guglielmo, about what happened within me. I couldn't bring myself to pray for a miracle, but even now, I wonder. A haunting question still lingers within me: What if I have not cooperated enough with grace, have not thought positively enough about my health and possible cure? Meetings to plan for the next five to ten years have been held at the university. I have found it hard to get interested in the discussions, because I don't believe I will be alive in five years. And thus the nagging questions: Am I being negative? Am I denying the power of prayer or closing myself to the possibility of healing? Do I *need* cancer in some way? I think, I hope, that I am being completely open to the positive, while trying to be realistic and honest. But I wonder, and I pray that I might live more in God.

Something needs to be said about causality and God's love, because how we understand the God-human relationship and the how and why of disease helps or hinders our movement toward peace. Miracles raise related questions about faith, the power of prayer, God's action in the world and why people suffer. Cancer often catalyzes questions about God's role in our suffering. We wonder about God's will. Even if we try to phrase our questions in ways that would not offend God, we often ask questions such as, "Why did God take him?" or "Why did God give her cancer?" and "Why does God let people suffer so?" Anyone dealing with suffering needs an appropriate understanding of God's role in it.

Suffering that is caused by human beings can be explained easily—harm done to others and to creation because of greed, anger, selfishness. But the question of suffering that cannot be explained still remains. What is God's role in suffering that results from disease or from the death of a loved one? Does God will these things? Does God will or somehow cause our suffering? Any answer depends on our understanding of how God acts in the world, which in turn depends upon our understanding of both God's love and our freedom. The image of God behind the comment "I don't understand God's will" and the understanding of God's action implicit in "You've got to accept God's will," conflict with the image of God presented in scripture—especially in the gospels.

The parable of the Prodigal Son in Luke offers a powerful image of God's love and our freedom. Here God is not omnipotent. There is no all-powerful father who punishes the child who does not respond to his love. In the parable the father does not force either son to respond in a certain way. The father loves unceasingly and forgives unconditionally, but he needs to wait patiently for his child's return. The parable presents a father whose powerful love gives birth, sustains life, offers forgiveness, effects healing; but also a parent whose boundless and non-coercive love waits, suffers, yearns and knows itself to be impotent, unable to change a child's heart, unable to force a return to heal that suffering; a father who continues to offer acceptance, love and forgiveness.

Every mother who sees her child suffer knows her love is impotent. She cannot remove the suffering; she cannot change her child's heart. But she continues to love boundlessly, unconditionally—powerfully sustaining life, offering forgiveness and effecting healing.

She continues to love passionately, desperately, even in the face of a life-threatening situation that she cannot change—suffering as she experiences her child's pain and her own impotence to remove it. This image better represents the God to whom I pray, the God in whom I believe. This is a God of infinitely powerful love that creates, sustains and empowers; a God of wonderfully non-coercive—and in that sense, impotent—love that yearns, awaits, suffers, accompanies, and ultimately—if and when the prodigal returns—embraces, heals and redeems.

Some people still ask why a God who's supposed to be *omnipotent* does not just remove all suffering. I believe that God created this world and each of us in freedom. Many things can go wrong with the process of creation. Some of my cells can start growing abnormally; this cancer within my body can even cause my death. I don't believe for a moment that God wills or wants me to have cancer. I believe that God loves me, loves all of us, and wants only our good—as a mother loves her child. But in creating and loving freely, God does not force us to do things; does not control the world from afar; does not make things happen. Rather, God created out of love, sustains us in love, and hopes for our good and our response to that love. Nevertheless, things can go wrong in the world, in the evolving process of creation.

In that sense I understand God as more like a mother who loves her child fully, unconditionally and freely. The mother wants only good for her child; she hopes that the child will grow in wisdom and grace. And so the mother watches as her child goes forth, runs and plays, enjoys good things, and she rejoices. But the mother also watches as her child falls and breaks a leg, and she too experiences pain. The mother suffers precisely because she loves her child so. It is because we love that we suffer. Just as my mother cried when we talked about my cancer, just as any mother suffers when she sees her child in pain, I believe that our God weeps and is the first to shed a tear when one of us suffers or dies. That understanding of God as compassionate Love, as one who suffers with and for us, helps me to deal with my cancer and with other people's suffering.

Another concept that has removed my anger and continues to help me find positive aspects along my journey is my understanding of the meaning of *good*. We grow up thinking that *good* means total peace or harmony—no suffering. But that is only one dimension of *good*. If it means only peace and the absence of conflict, the most *good* universe would consist of a single nonreactive element, like helium or another inert gas, so that nothing could go wrong. There would be no suffering because there would be no change. The world would be simple, unchanging—and boring.

Our world is complex and good because it involves intensity. There is more good in a plant than in a rock, in a human being than in a dog. There is also more good in a friendship in which two people share the depths of their hearts than in a superficial relationship.

The feelings and thoughts that we share, our intimacy and deep commitment create an intensity in our relationships that makes them good. But that intensity, a capacity that increases as the complexity of being increases, brings with it the possibility of disharmony. As complexity and intensity increase, so does the danger of something going wrong—rocks don't get cancer, rocks don't suffer with other rocks! Precisely because we love, we know less peace. When the people we love suffer, we suffer too. But we also live more intensely—and that is good.

I do not want to avoid friendships, avoid loving, avoid sharing intimately with people, so that I won't suffer when they suffer. It might bring more peace but less intensity. To become more human means to live and to love more intensely. We see in Jesus what it means to be fully human and fully divine: "No greater love than this, than to lay down one's life for a friend." Jesus loved intensely and did not avoid pain or suffering in his fierce and passionate commitment to love. We are born to eternal life precisely in and through loving intensely. That is what Francis meant when he proclaimed, "The love of him who loved us much is much to be loved."

The understanding that *good* comprises both harmony and intensity helps me to explain to others how my cancer can be a good. Not that I would choose cancer for myself or anyone else. But crises are good if they help us to see more clearly and to live more intensely. Brother Cancer has brought me not only pain and suffering; he has helped uncloud my vision of the essential and has called me to love more deeply. Thus, while he has decreased my "peace," he has increased my "intensity." And so, in some sense—however strange it sounds, however difficult to explain—he is good. That is why I do not want to be called a cancer survivor. I am not merely a survivor. I have walked with and grown through this cancer. I have been invited to live and to love more intensely by Brother Cancer.

I am not sure how to respond when people tell me they are praying for a miracle, praying that my cancer will be cured. I am grateful for their concern and appreciate their prayer. But I would ask their prayer only to help me to live the gospel, respond to God's love, and walk with Brother Cancer more faithfully. I do not want to go to Lourdes or to Padre Pio's shrine. At times I wonder why a physical cure seems to be the most important thing. Why do we not see the real miracles: a healing reconciliation between people who haven't spoken in years, a change of heart in someone who has been bitter and unhappy, a newly discovered enthusiasm and recommitment in someone's life, a changed perspective that offers a whole new way of seeing, an experience of love that frees one to accept death peacefully. When someone feels forgiven, senses grace, lives commitment, sees anew, finds peace—is that not a miracle?

As I walk now with Brother Cancer, the prayers of countless people accompany me. So many people have told me they are praying for me that I almost feel guilty about monopolizing so much prayer time. I even kid that I almost expect to hear an annoyed voice from the heavens asking, "Do you think you are the *only* person who needs attention?" So I do not walk alone with Brother Cancer; abundant love and constant prayer accompany me. I know that I must continue to walk with Brother Cancer, whether he is gentle or rough. There will be much struggle and pain, but I am certain there will also be much good and grace. I need wonder only *how* I will continue this journey with Brother Cancer, if I will remember the good, if I can remain open to God, and how I will respond to Brother Cancer's call to live more intensely.

Understanding
Unfinished

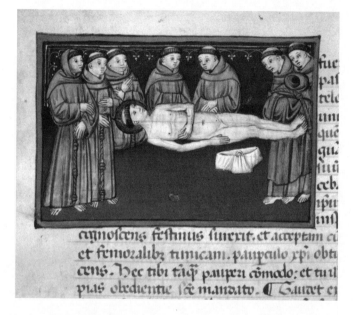

cognoscens festinus surrexit. et acceptam ei
et femoralibz tunicam. pauperilo xpi obtu
cens. Dec tibi tanq̃ pauperi comodo: et tuil
pias obediente sc̃e mandato. ⨂ Gaudet er

*Francis Welcoming Sister Death, Lying Naked on the
Naked Ground.*

Two years after the imprinting of the sacred stigmata
that is, in the twentieth year of his conversion,
under the many blows of agonizing illness,
he was squared like a stone to be fitted
into the construction of the heavenly Jerusalem,
and like a work of malleable metal
he was brought to perfection
under the hammering blows of many tribulations.

He asked to be taken to Saint Mary of the Portiuncula
so that he might yield up the spirit of life
where he had received the spirit of grace.

When he had been brought there, he showed by the example of Truth that he had nothing in common with the world. In that grave illness that ended all suffering, he threw himself in fervor of spirit totally naked on the naked ground so that in that final hour, when the Enemy could still rage, he might wrestle naked with the naked. Lying like this on the ground stripped of his sackcloth garment, he lifted up his face to heaven in his accustomed way, and wholly intent upon that glory, he covered with his left hand the wound in his right side, so that no one would see it. And he said to his brothers: "I have done what is mine; may Christ teach you yours."

...In all things
he wished without hesitation
to be conformed to Christ crucified,
who hung on the cross poor, suffering, and naked.

Naked he lingered before the bishop
at the beginning of his conversion;
and, for this reason,
at the end of his life,
he wanted to leave this world naked.
And so he charged the brothers assisting him,
under the obedience of love,
that when they saw he was dead,
they should allow him to lie naked on the ground
for as long as it takes to walk a leisurely mile.
O truly the most Christian of men,
who strove by perfect imitation to be conformed
while living to Christ living,
dying to Christ dying,
and dead to Christ dead,
and deserved to be adorned
with an expressed likeness!
…At last,
when all of the mysteries were fulfilled in him
and that most holy soul was released from the flesh
and absorbed into the abyss of the divine light,
the blessed man fell asleep in the Lord.
One of his brothers and followers saw that blessed soul
under the appearance of a radiant star
carried up on a shining cloud
to be borne aloft straight to heaven over many waters,
as if shining with the brightness of sublime sanctity
and filled with an abundance of heavenly wisdom and grace,
by which the holy man merited to enter
the place of light and peace
where he rests with Christ forever.
—Bonaventure, *Legenda maior*, XIV:3–6

On October 3 the Franciscan world celebrates the *Transitus*—the commemoration of the death of Francis. We call it the *Transitus* to show that we celebrate not his death but his "passing" from this life to the fullness of life. And so, not long ago, in the prayerful setting of our chapel I watched and listened as people reenacted the final hours of Francis's life with great drama and reverence.

That celebration of Francis's *Transitus* has become more special and meaningful for me, as my own image and understanding of Francis have changed over the years. The *Transitus* was always very powerful and prayerful for me, but during my early years in the order I had difficulty integrating different aspects of the life of the saint from Assisi. Early sources record a statement by Francis that is hard to understand or to accept, his admonition to his followers: *Let us begin again, for up to now we have done nothing.* Francis had done much: founded religious orders, touched countless lives, achieved intimacy with God. How could Francis not see or acknowledge his own goodness, his own accomplishments? How could he say he had done nothing, and at times even speak of himself as "wretched"?

Over the years Francis's words have begun to make sense. As I slowly and gradually have grown in my faith, my understanding of him has changed.

Earlier I didn't have the categories or experience to include a Francis who dared to say he had done nothing and who spoke of himself as miserable. Now I understand that he could see his own sin, his own nothingness more clearly as he progressed in his conversion, precisely because he drew nearer to God, lived more in that Light. Now I understand with Francis the unfinished emergence and eagerly make his words my own prayer: *Let us begin again, for up to now we have done nothing*.

Other words spoken by Francis months before his death have also come to make more sense to me. Shortly before his death, as he looked back on his life, Francis dictated his *Testament: The Lord gave me, Brother Francis, thus to begin doing penance in this way: for when I was in sin, it seemed too bitter for me to see lepers. And the Lord Himself led me among them and I showed mercy to them. And when I left them, what had seemed bitter to me was turned into sweetness of soul and body*.

Francis does not begin with an extraordinary, miraculous or mystical experience. Rather—what is intriguing if not astonishing, what is encouraging and inspiring for one who suffers—Francis talks about finding God in the ordinary, in the difficult and painful moments, in embracing the leper. In recent years this has become incredibly significant for me: In being with the leper, Francis came to know God's love. In encountering the other, Francis moved into deeper intimacy with God. His vision and the way he lived changed. In encountering the leper, Francis encountered God, and thus himself, in a new way. Somehow, the encounter enabled him to see his true self, his weak and sinful self, and to feel that self embraced by a loving and forgiving God. In seeing his own weakness and accepting his dependence on God, Francis became free. In knowing his own sin and becoming vulnerable, Francis could receive God's love and forgiveness. In the painful and difficult encounters of everyday ordinary life, Francis experienced grace; he tasted the presence of God as the bitter was changed into "sweetness of soul and body."

The accounts of Francis's death make sense to me now. He died as he had lived. Francis lived intensely, up to the moment of his death, even death itself. In his death we see what had been emerging throughout all of his life. In his death Francis finally completes the unfinished, the work-in-progress, the part that was his to do, his "painting without canvas."

Francis asked to be carried to the Porziuncola, where he had lived with his early companions; to be laid naked on the bare ground, wanting nothing to separate him from God; to have the Gospel of John that proclaimed service and littleness read to him. He gathered his followers, blessed them and encouraged them to do their part and to join him in praising God. In his death Francis lived what he had prayed earlier in his letter to the entire order: *Almighty, eternal, just and merciful God, give us miserable ones the grace to do for you alone what we know you want us to do and always to desire what pleases You. Inwardly cleansed, interiorly enlightened, and enflamed by the fire of the Holy Spirit, may we be able to follow in the footprints of Your beloved Son, our Lord Jesus Christ, and, by your grace alone, may we make our way to You, Most High, Who live and rule in perfect Trinity and simple Unity, and are glorified God almighty, forever and ever. Amen.*

Francis's prayer expresses his awareness of his sinfulness and dependence on God. It proclaims that God's grace is the source of all good, that we move through stages as we follow the Lord on our journey to the Father, that our lives are unfinished until we make our way to God the Most High. In his death, Francis reveals that his life is unfinished and helps us to understand his admonition, *Let us begin again, for up to now we have done nothing.*

Only now am I *beginning* to understand the unfinished. Only now is the power of the unfinished in Michelangelo's work becoming clear: the beauty, meaning, revelation in emergence. In his sculptures of the four slaves, Michelangelo powerfully presents the emergence of the person, the spirit becoming incarnate, the struggle to bring forth and give expression to what we are at our depths. In the sculpting of hard stone emerges the beauty of the spirit. In the painful struggle, in the emergence from the unfinished, is revealed the meaning of person and beauty of soul.

I can now see Francis as that rough-hewn stone. I understand that my own life is unfinished, expressed in its emergence. I begin to understand that we need to "begin again," that we are "unfinished" and always emerging—and that is the beauty. We need to continue to emerge, to live intensely, until we greet Sister Death, the unfinished celebrated in *transitus*.

Even the pain and suffering along the journey with cancer can be the sculpting of the stone of life from which emerges—slowly, imperceptibly—the spirit, the deepest truth of who we are, the more profound beauty, the presence of God. Before, I dismissed these "unfinished" works by Michelangelo as incomplete; I now understand how the unfinished in Michelangelo's art expresses the mystery of incarnation. And so Michelangelo's emerging slave symbolizes the spirit emerging in and through the stone, calls me to be attentive to my own emergence, challenges me to live and love intensely in the ordinary as the very sculpting and emerging of the spirit.

My encounter with cancer has also helped me to view my own death differently. Earlier, I had hoped that my death would be quick; I even expected it, because my father had died of a heart attack when he was fifty-five. I thought it would be a blessing to drop in my tracks on my way to teach a class. I always feared long, drawn-out illness. I wondered if I could handle being incapacitated, confined to bed. Much to my surprise, I now see how a long illness can be a time of grace, a time to rest in God and to come to know Christ crucified more intimately.

When I can think, pray and meditate, I can deal with the pain, so I usually refuse pain medication. I hate feeling fuzzy-brained, and it nauseates me. The doctors, nurses and most of my Franciscan brothers think I'm nuts—but it works for me. Francis came to know Christ crucified more intimately precisely in and through his own suffering, so I want to be open to that possibility. I don't want to lose the opportunity for deeper intimacy with God just to avoid physical pain. I want to live my death. I do not want to be drugged and numbed to my own suffering and that final visit of Sister Death. I believe that living my death is part of my response to Francis's admonition: "I have done what is mine to do; may Christ teach you what is yours to do."

When we are open to the experience of God's love, when we are vulnerable, when we can admit our sinfulness and know our dependence on God, then our vision, our life, our "painting" changes. Then our lives can proclaim with Francis "the love of him who loved us much is much to be loved." From the unhewn marble of our bodies emerges a graceful word of love. The more we struggle to find God in the ordinary, the more fully will we understand both the power and impotence of God's unconditional, non-coercive love. The power of God's impotent love will become known to us: The more we open ourselves to taste the bitter changed into sweet as we serve others, the more fully we will be able to embrace the cross. The more we seek to know Christ crucified in our suffering, the more we will be able to welcome Sister Death.

Cancer has been my leper, has helped me to see more clearly and to believe more deeply. And so I name and thank Brother Cancer. It has been difficult to explain this to others. Many who ask me how I am feeling seem unable or unwilling to hear my response. When I speak about my cancer, the prognosis, the pain and difficulty, many react by telling me that I will be fine. They either try to convince me that I will be cured by a miracle or that I should try another therapy. Others accept my condition, but when I say that my journey with cancer has been an experience of grace, they ask: "But how do you *really* feel?" Some cannot accept that cancer could have a positive side, and that I am not angry, distraught or depressed.

There are some with whom I can speak openly and honestly, who do not need to "remove" my cancer or change my response to it. A friend at the university, Barbara, has been that kind of friend, because she understands my experience. She herself was diagnosed with an aggressive cancer within a month of my diagnosis, and we have gone through operations and treatments at almost the same times. I visited her during one of her chemotherapy sessions—between my own treatments and weekly visits to the lab for blood work. Barbara listens gently, cares deeply, has laughed and cried with me, and always offers me a graceful, supportive presence that allows me to be myself.

Dave, a fellow Franciscan, has also given me that kind of acceptance. When we were at a provincial chapter meeting, he asked if we could take a walk together. Dave began by saying that he had heard conflicting reports about my health and wanted to hear directly from me. I related the story of the doctors finding metastatic cancer in my chest, the operation, the months of healing and the prognosis. Dave asked me about my spirit through it all. I talked about some of the graced moments, my desire to live more intensely, my difficulty in focusing on immediate tasks, my concern about continuing to walk with Brother Cancer and to do my part, my acceptance of my own death and my concern about predeceasing my mother.

We stopped walking. Dave placed his hands on my shoulders, and in a steady, gentle voice told me that he wanted to walk with me, wanted to be there for me however, whenever, wherever I might need him. My eyes welled with tears. I felt so incredibly cared for by my brother, by all my Franciscan brothers in that moment.

Dave then said that one of the reasons he had wanted to talk with me was that he was concerned that I might have lost focus. To explain what he meant, he shared an important story and image from his life. Before that day I hadn't even heard of a "range marker." However, the image truly spoke to my experience and so touched my heart that I have often returned to it during difficult moments.

Dave had been a fire-department chaplain. One day he was on a fireboat heading back to dock, when the officer on board told him to take the helm. The fireboat was large—over sixty feet and ninety tons—and Dave was afraid to pilot it. The officer pointed out a large pole on the shore with a flashing red light—a range marker—and instructed Dave to steer toward it. A short time later the officer pointed out a second range marker about three times taller, located 150 yards further in the distance, and told Dave to steer in the direction of the first range marker until it lined up with the second one. Then he explained: only when the two range markers merge and appear as one is the vessel where it is supposed to be—*in the channel*, on its proper course and headed safely into port.

Dave said he had been concerned that I might not line up my range markers, that I might be focused only on the future or only on the present, only thinking about death or only concerned with surviving cancer. After our talk, he said, he believed I had my range markers aligned. His words meant a lot to me, and his image continues to provide me with focus and challenge.

Although I believe I usually have my range markers aligned, there are times when I fear I focus only on the far distance. Sometimes I struggle to stay interested in conversations or to find energy to do things that appear superficial to me. I want to deal only with important, meaningful things. However, I need to muster energy for the more mundane tasks day to day. I want to keep focused on the distant range marker, the gift of eternal life offered to us beyond death. But I don't want to focus *only* on life beyond this life, on my death. I want to live this life ever more intensely, and so I want to continue to find energy for all the everyday tasks. I want to be occupied with what is essential. But whatever I need to do daily, I want to be able to find God within it, to keep aligned with my distant range marker. For I believe that our eternal life in God begins *now*, that we create who we are unto eternity, that we choose now to live either more or less in Love.

In his writings Francis speaks clearly about our choice: to see or to be blind, to live in the light of Love or to live in the dark of selfishness. Despite having read Francis's words and having studied his writings, I have only now begun, aided by Brother Cancer, to see how radical that choice is. Over the years I have accomplished things, touched lives and been a good person. But Brother Cancer has been trying to push me to see beyond that; to understand that my response to God's love must be radical, must come from my depths and involve my total being; to risk in faith and stand naked before God so that I might know God's love and forgiveness; to hazard being vulnerable and being led by the Lord so that I taste and see the glories of God and proclaim with my being that "the love of him who loved us much is much to be loved."

From a faith perspective this should be obvious because it is so essential. At some level I knew that our response to God's love must be *radical*—at the root of our being, determining who we become. Why did I need Brother Cancer to teach me how radical is that choice to live and love intensely? Why has it taken so long for me to see?

I fear that I won't respond fully just to avoid the pain of living and loving intensely. I fear not choosing radical intimacy with God just to remain in a familiar and comfortable life. I fear falling victim to images of our culture, to pressures to perform, to my own fear of the unknown—which might allow me to do good, to become popular, and even to know God somewhat, but which keep me from that deep love and intimacy for which my heart longs.

Brother Cancer showed me competing fears—the fear involved in surrendering and risking to live that intensely, and the fear that in refusing risk I might never know the intensity of love and intimacy with God. Brother Cancer taught me about the radical choice to love profoundly or just to exist—a choice best expressed in a story, best captured in an image.

When I was an undergraduate at Boston College, I did some volunteer work at the Walter E. Fernald School for the mentally and physically handicapped. A huge institution that served all of New England, it had about eight hundred residents. My work as a volunteer began with an orientation that included a tour. As we walked through the building designated for "Severely Retarded Males over 21," I noticed an odd door with a small window in it. The guide whisked our group down the corridor and up the stairs, but my curiosity drew me to linger and to peer through the window. I saw nothing except a puddle in the middle of the floor and some blankets thrown in a corner. I left the group and found a worker who could answer my questions. The story he shared with me symbolizes for me the radical choice: to live as before or to "paint" like Francis.

Under the blanket, huddled in the corner, hid a man who had been born deaf, mute and blind. His parents assumed he was retarded and left him at the institution as an infant. He had been there twenty years. Three times a day a staff member would shove food through the slot at the bottom of the door, and the man would devour it with animal ferocity. He did not use utensils to eat; he did not even wear clothes. He lived without human contact and had not been socialized; he urinated and defecated in his cell. Once a day someone would hose down both the man and his cell. Most of the day, he slept beneath the blankets. His existence was less than human.

The summer before my arrival, a Jesuit who worked as a volunteer in that building took it upon himself to care for the man. He attempted to reach out to that nameless man, to bring some human contact into his life. He had only *touch* as a means of communication. Slowly, gently, day by day, with a patience that bore grace, he "touched" him. He offered human contact—perhaps for the first time—and found, to the surprise of all, that the man was not mentally incompetent. Within weeks the Jesuit had led the man out of the building for walks on the grounds. In one short summer the naked, caged and isolated man had been clothed, freed, and had begun to relate to another human being. This human contact must have been terrifying at first, but it invited that man to a whole new world, to enter realms of experience that for years had been beyond his grasp and limited existence. For the first time in his life, he knew the warmth of the sun, the gentleness of a breeze, the strength given by a steady arm, and the graced touch of another human being.

At the end of that summer, the Jesuit returned to his studies, and because of a personnel shortage, no one could give the man individual attention. He reverted to his former state and again lay huddled in the corner under a blanket, a pool of urine in the center of his cell.

For one brief summer, a moment in his lifetime, that man born deaf, mute and blind had been invited to human existence. The Jesuit believed and imagined what others could not or dared not. His touch invited another human being to a radical new life, to an intimacy earlier unknown, to a life lived more intensely. The man needed to overcome his fears, to allow himself to be touched, to risk reaching out and becoming vulnerable. The man had to let go of the known and move beyond surviving, had to trust love and surrender to the encounter for the bitter to be turned into sweetness of soul and body.

Francis knew that our human experience could include radical intimacy with God. Brother Cancer has tried to teach me that the response is ours. We need to respond. We need to risk reaching out, being vulnerable, being led by the Lord to experience the bitter being turned into sweetness of soul and body. The choice is ours: blindness or sight; to remain within a cell of selfishness or to venture forth together to serve; to live superficially or to love intensely.

Brother Cancer has helped me to see that I can do good things and serve in the name of the gospel without experiencing the fullness and abundance of new life in God. Brother Cancer has invited me to see more clearly, to admit my own limitedness and dependence on God. Before, I took pride in my accomplishments, became attached to my reputation and thus remained within my cell. The touch of Brother Cancer beckoned me forth: he invited me to admit my absolute finitude and dependence; he gently led me and taught me to trust God's love, to taste God's goodness, and to see God's beauty.

It is difficult to maintain that intensity. As I have grown stronger, I have feared walking alone without Brother Cancer. I know that sounds strange; most people seek only to be "cancer free." It is not that I want the cancer to continue to spread, but I fear losing the experience of God that Brother Cancer has given me. If Brother Cancer were to leave at the end of my summer, would I revert to my life within my cell, would I still venture forth without the steadiness of his arm? Would I return to a hectic schedule of teaching and ministry, once again losing sight of my absolute dependence on God, or would I serve well, always aware of the good that God does through me? Would I be trapped again in consumer culture and become blind to my own selfishness, or would I live the mystery of the cross in dying to self, and so taste God's mercy, love and the fullness of life?

I am filled with questions and could continue, but I want to finish these pages tonight, for it seems appropriate to end my reflections on "how I got 'there,'" about my own "painting without canvas," on October 3, the day that we celebrate Francis's passing to the fullness of life.

Since I began journeying with cancer, since the first time the doctor told me that the cancer could be throughout my body in three to six months, since that first night that I thought about Sister Death, I have often heard echoing within me that refrain of Francis: "I have done what was mine to do, may Christ teach you what is yours to do." Since my cancer metastasized, I have wanted, felt a passion, sensed an urgency, to do what is mine to do. I have wondered much about what I am called to do. What is my part? I began to think that these words might be what was mine to do. I continue to hope that they might be helpful, but I now believe that this is but one small part of what I am meant to accomplish.

I hope that these reflections on my journey might help those who wonder how one can find peace with cancer. Trying to respond to the question of how I've found peace has helped me to look more closely at my own "painting," and I believe—I hope—to live more intensely, to paint with more awareness, passion, faith and intensity. It has been a blessing.

As I close, I am filled with gratitude but also with hope and fear. Celebrating Francis's *Transitus* this night, remembering a life of profound love, has filled me with gratitude for all those who have been words of love and grace in my life. But listening to Francis's song welcoming Sister Death also has engendered fear amid hope—recently, the doctors discovered a malignant tumor on my liver. I hope that I might sing with Francis, might reach out and more fully embrace this leper called cancer, might overcome my fears and seek only to love and to serve, might risk being led by the Lord and so come to taste the sweetness of soul and body.

I see more clearly now what is mine to do—not to finish these pages, but to complete my painting without canvas. My part involves walking with Brother Cancer, living what he has taught me, following faithfully in the footprints of our Lord Jesus Christ, admitting my sinfulness and weakness, seeking to love and to serve, becoming vulnerable before my God, living and loving, painting with my life until that final brush stroke, living even my death so that I may welcome the sister who beckons me, not to death but to the fullness of life.

I hope to continue painting, to hone my technique, to keep my range markers aligned, to listen more attentively, to embrace more fully and walk more gracefully with Brother Cancer. I pray passionately that I might "do what is mine to do," that I might proclaim that "the love of him who loved us much is much to be loved." I pray that your own living, your own painting without canvas, might continue to reveal and ever more clearly express life, love, and God.